NEWCASTLE AND TYNESIDE IN THE SECOND WORLD WAR

Northumberland Army Cadet Force Detachment, Lime Street, Newcastle, April 1943.

The People's Story

by Neil R Storey & Fiona Kay

© Neil R Storey & Fiona Kay, 2020
ISBN: 978-0-9503178-7-8

All rights reserved. No part of this book may be reproduced, stored or introduced into a retrieval system or transmitted in any way or by any means (electronic, mechanical, photocopying, recording or otherwise) without the prior permission of the publishers.

The opinions expressed in this book are those of the author.

Published by:
City of Newcastle Upon Tyne
Newcastle Libraries
Tyne Bridge Publishing, 2020
www.tynebridgepublishing.org.uk

This book is dedicated to the memory of Dorothy Kay and the thousands of children like her who were evacuated from their homes in Newcastle and Tyneside during the Second World War.

Design: Derek Tree
Editor: Vanessa Histon
Photographs supplied by
Newcastle City Council
NCJ Media
Neil R Storey's Photo Archive
Fiona Kay Collection

Front cover: The Drums of the Royal Artillery from Debdon Drill on the march at Heaton, 1941

Commemorative Map showing many of the services and the role Northumberland played during the Second World War, devised by Donald McCullough, it is one of a series produced for the counties of England in 1946

CONTENTS

Introduction....................6
The Inter-War Years..............8
Evacuees........................15
Air Raid Precautions............22
Air Raids.......................38
The Military...................50
The Merchant Navy..............80
The Home Guard.................84
Aliens and Spies...............96
Women War Workers.............103
Land Girls....................108
Life on the Home Front........114
Victory!......................127
Appendices....................131
Bibliography..................150

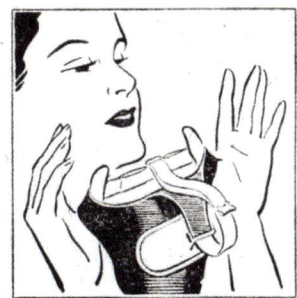

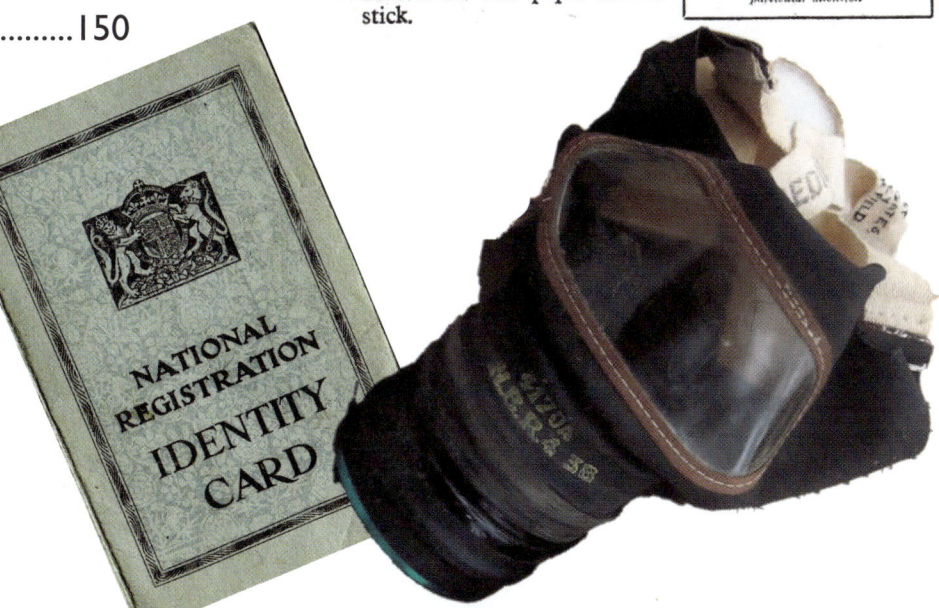

INTRODUCTION

When writing or discussing the First World War, historians and authors often speak of *'that remarkable generation'* and *'a generation passed'*. Statistically that was almost the case, but that generation was not entirely wiped out, and neither were their children, despite Spanish 'flu and the hard times of the interwar years that claimed more lives than the Great War itself. For those of us who come from the post-1945 generations it is hard to imagine how it must have felt for all those who had gone through so much to face the prospect of, and to live through, a Second World War. This time there would be air raids, the like of which were unprecedented in the experience of the British people. After the Dunkirk evacuation and the fall of France we also faced a clear and present danger of invasion by enemy forces that could have led to a terrifying occupation by Nazi Germany. This would have inflicted repression and horror on our people as it had done in the countries it had already occupied in Europe.

To combat the Nazi menace conscription was introduced in 1939 and thousands of men were called-up for military service in the armed forces. From 1941 women also faced conscription and the men and the women of Newcastle and Tyneside were not backwards in coming forward to volunteer to *'do their bit'*, even before they received their papers for compulsory service. Indeed, Newcastle was the very first British city to fill its entire quota for its Territorial Army units months before the outbreak of war and requests were made that they be allowed to recruit more. The organisations that operated under the Air Raid Precautions scheme, such as Wardens, Rescue Crews, First Aid Parties, Auxiliary Fire Service, Women's Voluntary Service, British Red Cross Society and St John Ambulance, had thousands already trained by September 1939 and a superbly planned and practised emergency response system had also been established. Even more people joined up and rallied to the call for Local Defence Volunteers (later retitled the Home Guard) when Britain faced its darkest hours in 1940.

Those who remained at home did not just sit, worry and mope. Newcastle and Tyneside raised millions of pounds for war charities and the war effort and, in 1940, Newcastle raised more money for the Red Cross and St John 'Penny a Week' fund than anywhere else in the country. A host of other local and national war charities benefited from the generosity of the people of Newcastle and Tyneside, not least the Northumberland and Durham War Needs Fund. Women, young lads and old men built a mighty workforce to take the place of those who left for war service and provided the man- and woman-power in the shipyards, factories and on the land that was so desperately needed in wartime. Then, after a long day at work they would often go and take their turn on duty with one of the ARP services, many of them taking their knitting with them to make comforts such as gloves, socks, scarves and balaclavas for service personnel.

Such was the 'wartime spirit.' It would be naive to say everyone pulled their weight and got on together, but to go against the grain was certainly more unusual than it had been in peacetime. Above all, if people did not work together for the war effort they were seen as unpatriotic! Numerous times during the war many people were very grateful for small but kind gestures from others that helped them through some very dark times.

At the moment the Second World War is only narrowly hanging on in the national curriculum for schools. Those of us who grew up in the last quarter of the 20th century were the last generation to have the chance of really knowing those who lived through the war years. We were able not just to sit with one person but to get involved in groups and reunions, to hear the stories they had to tell with their pals around them putting them right if they went wrong (or memory failed) or offered different perspectives on events and experiences on the home front or in the forces. It was usually possible to tell who had been the regular soldiers, indeed, the high regard placed on those who had been pre-war 'regulars' by those who had joined 'for the duration' or had been conscripted was still a very palpable thing even decades after the end of the war. Moreover, one could never fail to be moved by the respect they had for their fallen comrades and for those who had been taken as prisoners of war, especially those who had been in Japanese hands.

Sadly the generation that saw uniformed service in the Second World War are, like all old soldiers, fading away. Even children who were evacuees in 1939 are now in their eighties and we are losing them too. Many of those who did serve in the Second World War often didn't talk about it to their families. Geordies and Tynesiders are modest folk and what may seem to us remarkable achievements are shrugged off as something they had to do and they simply got on with it. Many history books focus on the blitz on London in 1940 and there is little or nothing said about the ordeal Tyneside went through in 1941 when the area became a target for bombing raids that created infernos with columns of flames that could be seen for miles around shooting high in the night sky. Factories, shops, homes and even air raid shelters were reduced to rubble and hundreds of people, young and old, lost their lives.

This book does not claim to be encyclopaedic; there have been some superb volumes written on the wartime history of Newcastle and Tyneside and there are also some excellent online resources. What we have set out to do is find the stories, important achievements, military units, heroes, significant events and incidents in Newcastle and Tyneside that many would not be aware of or that had significant impact on the area and lingered in the memories of local people. No doubt there will be more to find and some we will never know about. There is a danger that among future generations the Second World War, the lessons that can be learned from it and the profound impact it had on the ordinary people of Britain will become more distant, remote and, to some, sadly, irrelevant. We hope this book, which includes many previously unpublished images from our personal collections, images kindly loaned for the book from precious family albums and the remarkable archives of Newcastle Libraries, will be a useful starting point and a small tribute to the lads and lasses of the Toon and Tyne who gave their all during the Second World War.

The concluding words of the Newcastle's Victory Celebrations souvenir booklet, published in 1946, are particularly poignant with this in mind and are now, all these years later, are just as appropriate:

'As we in Newcastle turn over memory's pages we recapture the indomitable spirit of those breathless days. In a spirit of thankfulness it is good that we should remember.'

Neil Storey and Fiona Kay
Northumberland
2019

THE INTER-WAR YEARS

The River Tyne with Newcastle in the background from the top of Spillers wharf while it was still under construction, May 1937

Times were tough for the men who returned from the Great War and the 1920s were beset with unemployment and lay-offs in the North East. Veterans associations were formed to keep up the comradeship they had known during the conflict and to help those on hard times or those who had suffered life changing injuries get the pensions they deserved. Training schemes teaching practical skills were set up in Newcastle and Tyneside to help men retrain. The Housing Act of 1919 made good-quality housing and living conditions a national responsibility and Prime Minister David Lloyd George set local authorities the task of building 500,000 new homes within three years *"to make Britain a fit country for heroes to live in"* Many local men found work labouring in the clearances of Newcastle slums and on the construction of council housing 'homes for heroes' on the Pendower Estate in the west and Walker in the east, followed by developments in areas such as Dinnington, Walker and Shieldfield.

As the country began to find its feet again employers began to expand, notably Angus Watson who opened a fish canning factory on City Road. By 1928 he was employing 10,000, no wonder he become known as 'The Sardine King'. Major engineering works in the city

Pottery Bank at the rear of Ropery Walk, Walker, shortly before its clearance to make way for new housing c1935. Right: Angus Watson, famed for their tinned fish, brought much-needed employment to Newcastle during the hard times between the wars

We Are Fighting—

NO Guide to the Exhibition is complete without reference to the great Tyneside organisation of Angus Watson & Co. Ltd. We are fighting for new industries on Tyneside, and we have built one at the City Road Preserving Works, where " SAILOR " SAVOURIES and " SAILOR " SOUPS are made !

Visit it—the net-work of its culinary marvels is laid open to your inspection at Angus Watson and Company's Stands, 142 and 147. Many wonderful Ready-to-Serve foods are served you free in the parlour.

ANGUS WATSON AND CO. LTD.

'READY TO SERVE at STANDS 142/7, Avenue E.

SKIPPERS, MY LADY FRUITS, SAILOR SAVOURIES, SAILOR SOUPS, MY LADY CRAB, SAILOR SALMON AND SARDINES.

—And Winning

created more jobs; the greatest of these projects being the construction of the Tyne Bridge, officially opened by King George V on 10 October 1928.

The publicity for the bridge was followed up with the North-East Coast Exhibition, a world's fair to showcase the engineering skills, industries, trade and arts of Newcastle, the Tyne and the Wear. It was staged on Exhibition Park between May and October 1929 and was attended by an average of 30,000 visitors a day. The problem was that times were not right for further expansion because the world was entering a period now known as 'The Great Depression.' The knock-on effects of the crash of the American stock market sent international trade into a tail spin it would take years to recover from. Men wanted to work but if there was no work to be had many lads remained on the dole and some families were reduced to living in biting poverty.

Whenever times are hard some people will be drawn towards those who offer to improve their lot and Tyneside became a fruitful recruiting ground for both Socialists and Fascists. Following the formation of the British Union of Fascists (BUF) in 1932 by Sir Oswald Mosley, the 'Blackshirts' quickly picked up recruits in Newcastle. They began holding open-air propaganda meetings; one of the earliest was at Marlborough Crescent bus station where they arrived mob handed and with a lorry to use as a stage. The speaker bore an uncanny likeness to Hitler and, after haranguing him for a while, the onlookers had heard enough and turned the lorry over. Labour groups such as The National Unemployed Workers Movement led anti-fascist opposition but many ordinary people of Newcastle also acted against the Fascists and there were a number of clashes and a protest march was organised when Mosley attempted to speak at a rally on the Town Moor in 1934.

The engineering marvel of its day, the Tyne Bridge nearing completion in 1928

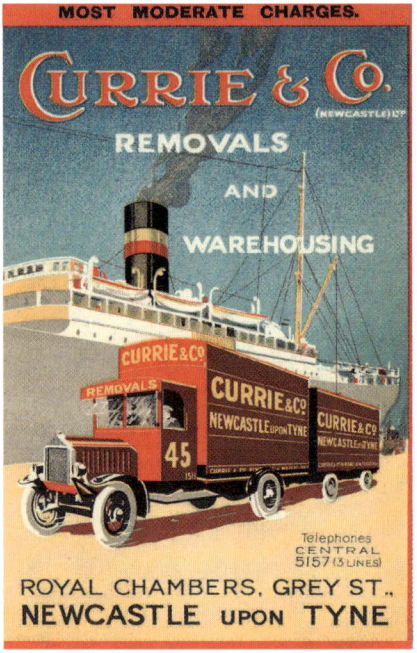

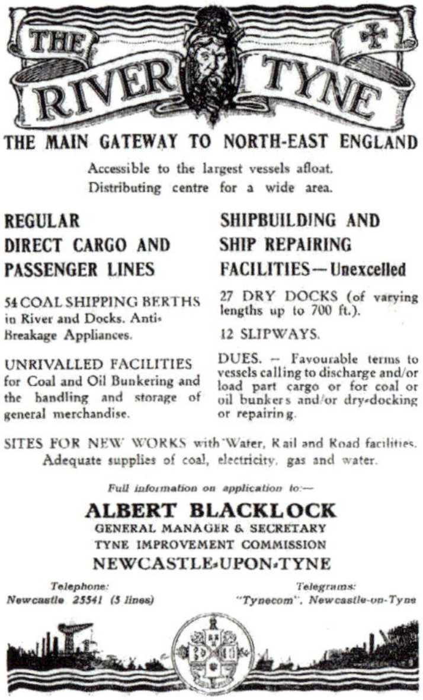

Jarrow Crusaders on their march to London in 1936

In 1936 another march attracted the interest of the national press. Some 200 local men or 'Crusaders' decided to protest about the unemployment and poverty in Jarrow and marched to London carrying a petition for the re-establishment of Palmer's shipyard, which had been the major employer in the town. Through rain and shine they marched behind the Jarrow Crusade banner, led by harmonica players, as many of them had marched in the Great War, except this time they were wearing flat caps instead of helmets. The 'Crusaders' did not get their wish, Palmer's was not reinstated and many of the 'Crusaders' felt their march had been a failure. Even so the images of the march rapidly became established as icons of working-class struggle. Long-term the Jarrow Crusade has become regarded by historians as a defining moment of the 1930s that was not forgotten when social reforms were addressed in the years after 1945.

Despite the hardship on Tyneside, there were campaigns to provide food and ambulances for Spain during the Spanish Civil War in 1937. Over 100 of the anti-fascists from Newcastle and Tyneside who had faced down the local Blackshirts went on to join the International Brigade fighting the fascists in Spain. Among them was Frank Graham, who joined the

Invitations being sent out to attend the North East Coast Exhibition, 1929

Tyne Electrical Engineers recruits marching to St Thomas's Church, Newcastle, May 1939

British Battalion and fought in the bloody battle of Jarma in 1937. Frank will be best remembered for his local history publications during the 1970s and 80s. Frank himself was wounded and twenty-four of his comrades from the North East lost their lives in the conflict.

In 1938 Hitler ordered his forces to occupy the Sudetenland and major concerns were felt across Europe about what he might do next. British Prime Minister Neville Chamberlain flew to Munich to see if some form of non-aggression agreement could be reached. Meanwhile, plans for the evacuation of children were made, Territorial Army (TA) units were put into a state of readiness for mobilization and the British public received their first issue of gas masks. When Chamberlain returned he declared he had secured 'Peace in our time.' Chamberlain, however, had only bought Britain time and on 2 March 1939 the authorities announced that the TA was to be doubled in size. Many TA officers thought that this late expansion was deplorable and really should have been addressed in the mid-1930s when the Nazis began to militate the German people and rebuild their armed forces on an ever-growing scale. The TA began training units in Anti-Aircraft (AA) gunnery and searchlight defence, but rather than expand the TA to accommodate this, units of Yeomanry, Royal Field Artillery and even infantry were converted over to AA including 5th Battalion, Royal Northumberland Fusiliers (TA) with their headquarters at Walker, which became a searchlight battalion.

When expansion was granted some TA companies welcomed plenty of new volunteers but others found the men from their local towns were far more reticent, as reported in the *St George's Gazette*, the Journal of the Northumberland Fusiliers on 31 March 1939:

Cover of the programme for the Military Display and exhibition staged on the Town Moor, June 1938

'X' Company's vigorous recruiting campaign at Hexham continues. Officers have been seen at the dead of night surreptitiously sticking up posters on various private properties. Heavy mail bags of personal letters to the youth of the town have issued from the Orderly Room. 'Personal contact' has become the slogan of Major Seth-Smith and his officers. It is said that people have been stopped in the street while entering shops and leaving cinemas. but such is the apathy of sections of modern youth that they flee like rabbits to their burrows on the approach of an officer along the street. In fact, the Company Commander, entering a grocer's for 1lb of butter, could not get served as all the assistants had fled in alarm to the back-shop.

On 17 May local newspapers proudly reported that the Lord Mayor had received a telegram from Mr Leslie Hore-Belisha, The Secretary of State for War, congratulating Newcastle on being the first place in England to recruit all its Territorial Army units up to full strength. In response, Sir Robert Aske, MP for Newcastle East, asked the War Minister to allow Newcastle to raise a third line of Territorials in the city.

On 26 May the Military Training Act 1939 (often referred to as 'The Militia Act') was passed by Parliament. It was our country's first peacetime act of conscription and applied to all males aged between twenty and twenty-one. It required 35,000 men to serve for six months' full-time military training. After this they would be transferred to the Reserve for three and a half years, during which time they 'might be recalled in an emergency for full time duty.' In reality most of these lads, commonly known as 'Militiamen', were still in uniform when war broke out and they were in 'for the duration.'

The glorious summer of 1939 was blessed with the finest warm weather, very much as it had been over the summer of 1914. There was no doubt that war would be declared – it was just a question of when - and people wanted to make the best of what peacetime was left. Old hands recalled that Territorial Army summer camps of 1939 were filled with training that seemed more purposeful than before and those who had recently joined up were assessed for promotion potential. Many a good young soldier came away with his first stripe, and by the time of the outbreak of war some of them had even made Sergeant or been selected for officer training.

The golden sands of the North-East, however, were darkened during August 1939 by the sinister cigar-shaped shadow cast by the Graf Zeppelin II (LZ 130) moving slowly along the coast. Most of those who saw it believed that its intentions were malevolent and their suspicions were later to be confirmed. The Graf

Building a sandbag wall around a public building in Newcastle to protect it from bomb splinters and absorb blast, September 1939

Zeppelin was reconnoitring the tall radio towers that had been erected along the North Sea Coast from Portsmouth to Scapa Flow.

August Bank holiday had been dubbed 'silver wedding weekend', because the many couples who married during the month of the outbreak of the Great War were now celebrating 25 years of marriage. The rush to wed on the eve of war was no different in 1939. Many prospective bridegrooms who were expecting a possible call-up notice had to cancel their honeymoons; among them was Territorial soldier Gordon Stout, who married Miss Jessie Scott at Whitley Bay on the afternoon of 25 August but instead of a honeymoon in the Lake District he had to rejoin his searchlight battalion of The Royal Northumberland Fusiliers the following day.

Mounting international tensions saw Chief Constables issue mobilization notices to all members of the Observer Corps on 24 August 1939. On 25 August Hitler invaded Poland and Britain stepped up to a war footing. Over the previous days holidays were already being cancelled for staff in banks and some of the bigger offices, many public buildings were already belted around with sandbag walls and their window panes crossed with rubberised tape to reduce flying glass in the event of a bomb blast. Policemen were on duty with their service respirators in their issue bags slung over their shoulders and with their blue shrapnel helmets, stencilled POLICE in white lettering, carried over the gas mask bag. Territorial Army 'key parties' assembled at their drill halls and set about building sandbag blast walls and digging shelter trenches; the officers ensured all paperwork was in order and procedures in place and tested for mobilization. They did not have long to wait.

EVACUEES

Rehearsal for evacuation at Cowgate Schools, Newcastle, 29 August 1939

In January and February 1939 Local Authorities in Reception Areas began the search for potential foster homes for evacuees. Volunteers, described as Visitors, interviewed householders and filled in census forms. These returns were to help decide how many evacuees could be billeted in each area. Newcastle Education Authority's arrangements for the evacuation of 45,000 schoolchildren were announced in April 1939. A mass of equipment had already been prepared, including a badge for every child, a linen label to be tied loosely round the child's neck and tucked under their upper garment, a banner of each school party and thousands of armlets for the teachers and other adults assisting in the evacuation.

To simplify administration, each school was given a number that would be used on all their labels, banners and tags. The badge issued to each child bore the letters N.C.T. (for Newcastle) to help with the rapid identification of children who may stray and get lost

Poster for the evacuation, August 1939

from their party. The badges came in a variety of colours and shapes to minimise any confusion that may occur when different schools were using the same station, e.g. NCT 31 would have a circular badge, NCT 32 would have a semi-circle, NCT 33 a diamond and NCT 34 a hexagon. Each label would display the child's name, home address, school and school number written in Indian ink. Some parents went so far as to have cheap bracelets engraved with their child's name and home address.

City and County of Newcastle upon Tyne.

Evacuation of School Children and certain other Persons in the event of a War Emergency.

1. It is necessary that the contents of this notice should be known to EVERY CITIZEN OF NEWCASTLE UPON TYNE.

2. Do not be alarmed because this notice has been sent to you. We do not claim to have any more information than you regarding the international situation ; we do not know whether the arrangements to secure the removal of the children and other persons needing special care to a less crowded place will ever be used ; we earnestly hope that they will not ; but for the sake of the children and of the others needing special care we must all be prepared. Better arrangements can be made in the calmness of peace than in the anxiety of war.

3. It is not an easy job for the teachers and officials of the City, the railway companies, the traffic commissioner and the bus companies to arrange for over forty thousand school children to be removed in a single day to less crowded districts where they may be housed, fed and educated, and for about the same number of other persons needing special care to follow them the next day. It is very public-spirited of the officials, teachers and other friends in the less crowded areas to make billeting and educational arrangements for the benefit of our citizens and children, and of householders in those areas to receive our dear ones into their homes.

4. Before the time fixed for the return of the forms enclosed, meetings of parents will be held in the schools, when fuller information will be given and questions may be asked.

5. If you still find it hard to understand anything in this notice, talk it over with your wife (husband) and friends or call at the nearest school where the head teacher will gladly welcome you and will be ready as always, to do all he (she) can to help you.

6. So we ask you to give us the information we seek. By doing so quickly and carefully you will be helping yourself, your families and your friends, as well as those whose public duty it is to undertake urgently a task of great magnitude and difficulty.

WILLIAM R. WALLACE, Lord Mayor.
GEORGE DIXON, Sheriff.
JOHN ATKINSON, Town Clerk and Evacuation Officer.
THOMAS WALLING, Director of Education and Schools' Evacuation Officer.

Covering note from the City and County of Newcastle explaining the importance of returning the forms it accompanied to enable those eligible to register for the evacuation scheme, August 1939

Each school would display a banner at the front of its 'marching column' and even the arm bands worn by teachers and helpers were colour coded: Green for school party leaders, yellow for department heads or company leaders and white for assistant teachers and voluntary helpers. There were also red armlets marked NCT DO for district office staff and blue ones lettered NCT HQ for headquarters staff. Every teacher was also issued with a small first aid kit and arrangements were made in the event of an evacuation for the heads of schools from poorer areas of the city to be provided with a communal bag of rations to be used for the benefit of more needy cases.

Evacuee children from Newcastle arriving at the Archbold Hall, Wooler 1, September 1939

Soon after the announcement every Newcastle household with a child of school age was sent a circular and a further 65,000 more copies were sent out to citizens in general over the following week. With each of these pamphlets were two forms, one pink, to be filled in respect of school children and the other in buff colour to be filled in for all other people to be evacuated, specifically expectant mothers, women with children under five years of age, blind adults and adults with severe disabilities. Newspapers urged people who had not received the pamphlets to get in touch with the City Education Office or the Town Hall. Meetings for concerned parents were held at schools across the city where school heads would answer questions about the scheme.

On 24 August school teachers were recalled from their summer holidays and thrown in to preparations for the 'go' signal. The first appeal appeared in the Newcastle newspapers for volunteers with motor cars for the evacuation of children 'in the event of national emergency' from Grey Court Convalescent Home Riding Mill; patients from Castle Hill Convalescent Home, Wylam and patients from the Royal Victoria Infirmary. Over the following days the parents of Newcastle schoolchildren received yellow cards and instructions as to the place and time they had to assemble with their kit, a day's supply of food and gas masks for evacuation.

A huge evacuation rehearsal was staged in Newcastle on 29 August, involving thousands of local children who did not have to wait long to experience the real thing. On 31 August 1939 the dreaded order was sent out by the Ministry of Health: 'Evacuate Forthwith' and at 8.30am on 1 September 1939 the first contingent of schoolchildren to be evacuated from Newcastle steamed out on a packed train from the Central Station. When they left the children had no idea who they would be staying with. On 2 September 1939 a further 12,818 Newcastle mothers and children under school age were also evacuated. By the evening of 2 September some 50,000 children from Newcastle and Gateshead were evacuated to safer areas in Northumberland, Cumberland, Westmorland, Durham County and the North Riding of Yorkshire.

A number of children were also privately evacuated directly to friends and members of extended family who lived in safe areas of the countryside. Some children were even sent abroad. The Children's Overseas Reception Board (CORB) evacuated 2,664 children overseas from Britain; 1,532 were sent to Canada; 576 to Australia; 353 to South Africa and 203 to New Zealand. An estimated 11,000 children also went abroad by private arrangement; over 6,000 to Canada and the remainder to the United States. Letters from children evacuated overseas occasionally appeared in the local press and they seemed to be treating the experience as a great adventure.

These journeys were fraught with danger and the vessels carrying evacuees faced the same perils as any others during the war. The case of the SS *Volendam* should have been taken as a warning. On 23 August 1940, while heading into the Atlantic on her way to Canada with 320 children aboard, including twenty Newcastle evacuees, she was torpedoed by the German submarine U-60. The Captain gave the order to abandon ship. Despite the sea being rough, all the lifeboats got away safely and all passengers and evacuees were soon picked up by the other merchant vessels in their convoy. The evacuees returned to Newcastle by train on 4 September wearing springs of white heather in their button holes and tags pinned to their coats bearing a congratulatory message and praise for their bravery from Geoffrey Shakespeare, Dominions Under Secretary. All the children appeared to be in high spirits. Among them was Irene Lattimer of Wingrove Road, who had her birthday on the boat the day they were torpedoed. She commented 'A nice birthday present I got from Hitler wasn't it?' Quite undaunted, she said she still wanted to go to Canada. Geoffrey Cowan of Plessey Terrace, High Heaton, had been in his bare feet when he was taken on deck and to the lifeboats and was also still willing to go. The youngest evacuee was Kenneth Campbell (6) of High Heaton; when asked if he wanted to go to Canada he simply replied 'I want to go home.'

Things did not go so well for the *City of Benares*. She had steamed out of Liverpool bound for Canada with a group ninety evacuee children, including a party of eleven children from Wearside, and ten adult escorts. On 13 September 1940 she was 600 miles out in the North Atlantic when she was torpedoed by the German submarine U-48 and sank with the loss of 121 crew, five adults and seventy-seven children. Only two of the eleven Wearside kids survived, one was Eleanor Wright (13) and the other was Billy Short (9) who's little brother Peter was in sick bay with measles and was lost. Among the adult dead was the well-known local figure, Alderman William Golightly of Gosforth, President of the Northumberland Miners Association.

The tragic sinking of the *City of Benares* brought a halt to the overseas evacuation of children. The few crew and children who survived the sinking, some of them from the North East, were haunted by the experience for the rest of their lives.

For many children, evacuation to safe areas in the countryside of northern Britain was also an adventure, but the novelty soon wore off. There had been no bombings and the war seemed a very distant affair so, as Christmas approached, local authorities arranged visits for groups of mothers to see their children and thousands of them returned home again to Newcastle and Tyneside to spend the festive season with their families. So many children came home that the Home Office issued warnings in newspapers and on posters telling mothers to leave their children where they were, but by 21 October 1939 11,000 evacuated children had returned to their Tyneside homes. Consequently, after the fall of France in 1940 there was a second evacuation, especially away from coastal areas of the east and south coast where there was a danger of invasion forces landing. In Newcastle 10,000 children and a further 3,000 at Gateshead were registered for the evacuation carried out on 7-8 July 1940. Schoolchildren were also evacuated from Tynemouth borough, Jarrow, Hebburn, Felling, Whickham and Sunderland.

Evacuation did not end there, Newcastle followed the example of Birmingham by requisitioning about 100 of the largest empty houses in the area and converting them into hostels for the temporary use of families made homeless by enemy action. In addition to the hostels, in November 1939 William Gray, Newcastle's chief billeting officer, announced he had a further 16,000 billets in occupied houses ready to help homeless families. Children from London, Coventry and other bombed cities and towns also came to live in Newcastle from the autumn of 1940 onwards. Many had little more than the clothes they stood up in and a special appeal was made by the Lord Mayor (Councillor A.D. Russell) for blankets for them. An appeal was made for prams so evacuee mothers could take their young children out for fresh air. After the initial return of our local evacuees in 1939 there were further evacuations over the next few years, notably during the invasion scares of 1940 and during the bombing of Tyneside in 1941.

As the Allies made successful landings in Normandy on 6 June 1944, Nazi Germany sought vengeance by launching V1 flying bombs, commonly known as 'Doodlebugs' on London seven days later. In September the first V2 rockets fell on London and families fled out of the capital and its suburbs again. On Monday 17 July 1944, Newcastle took in 127 families consisting of

Children from South Shields evacuating to the countryside in July 1941

nearly 800 mothers and children from London, Hendon, Rochester and Croydon. The Civil Defence organisation and Women's Voluntary Service (WVS) canvassed residential areas to help identify homes to take evacuees and turned out in force to help look after luggage and escort evacuees to their billets. On arrival many were bussed over to Whickham View School, West End, where over 200 women and children were examined by the Assistant Medical Officer of Health for Newcastle. An excellent report of health was returned and the evacuees were bussed to their billets. The people of Heaton were especially generous in offering their homes. Mrs A C Clark, a WVS Billeting Officer, said: *'I can only describe the reception as absolutely wonderful. Householders were coming out into the street to meet the buses carrying the mothers and children and taking them off into their homes where they had tea and food waiting.'* Equally, all those who had been evacuated were amazed at the warmth of the welcome that the people of Heaton had given them. Recreational and educational facilities were

A certificate of appreciation recording the message from Queen Elizabeth, sent to those who provided homes for evacuees in 1939

made available to the adult 'visitors' from London and YMCA 'welcome clubs' were provided for evacuated mothers at Newcastle, Byker, West Newcastle, Walker and Welbeck Estate, Gateshead, Jarrow, South Shields, Sunderland (Burdon Road and Ford Estate), North Shields, Howdon, Wallsend, Blyth, Blaydon and Chopwell. With enquiries mounting to nearly 400 a day at the Central Information Bureau for evacuees in Newcastle Town Hall. they had to move to bigger premises in the Durant Hall, Ellison Place (off Northumberland Street).

In November 1944, 200 Newcastle evacuees, along with 200 more from South Shields and Wallsend formed the last organised party of evacuees to be brought back home for good. Many returned from foster homes in Cumberland and Westmorland for the first time after five years away. They arrived at Central Station in a specially chartered train where china dolls and wooden Tommy Guns and the like were priority baggage. They were taken to Rutherford College where parents were waiting and there were many tearful reunions. The Newcastle they returned to seemed strange to many of them - they had left as toddlers and returned as youngsters, some had forgotten what trams looked like, some even had the unmistakable hint of a Cumberland accent.

'I can only describe the reception as absolutely wonderful. Householders were coming out into the street to meet the buses carrying the mothers and children and taking them into their homes where they had tea and food waiting.'

The first party of evacuees to return to Southern England with official sanction left Newcastle station on 13 December 1944. A *Newcastle Journal* reporter asked three of them about their feelings at leaving Tyneside, Eileen Wilcox (13) of Maidstone, Kent; Derek Hayes (13) of Uckfield, Sussex and Mrs Heppell of Portsmouth all spoke very highly of the people and children they had got to know, they liked the big shops and were only too grateful to have been able to get away from the bombs but they all missed the fruit they were able to get back home and the warmer weather.

AIR RAID PRECAUTIONS

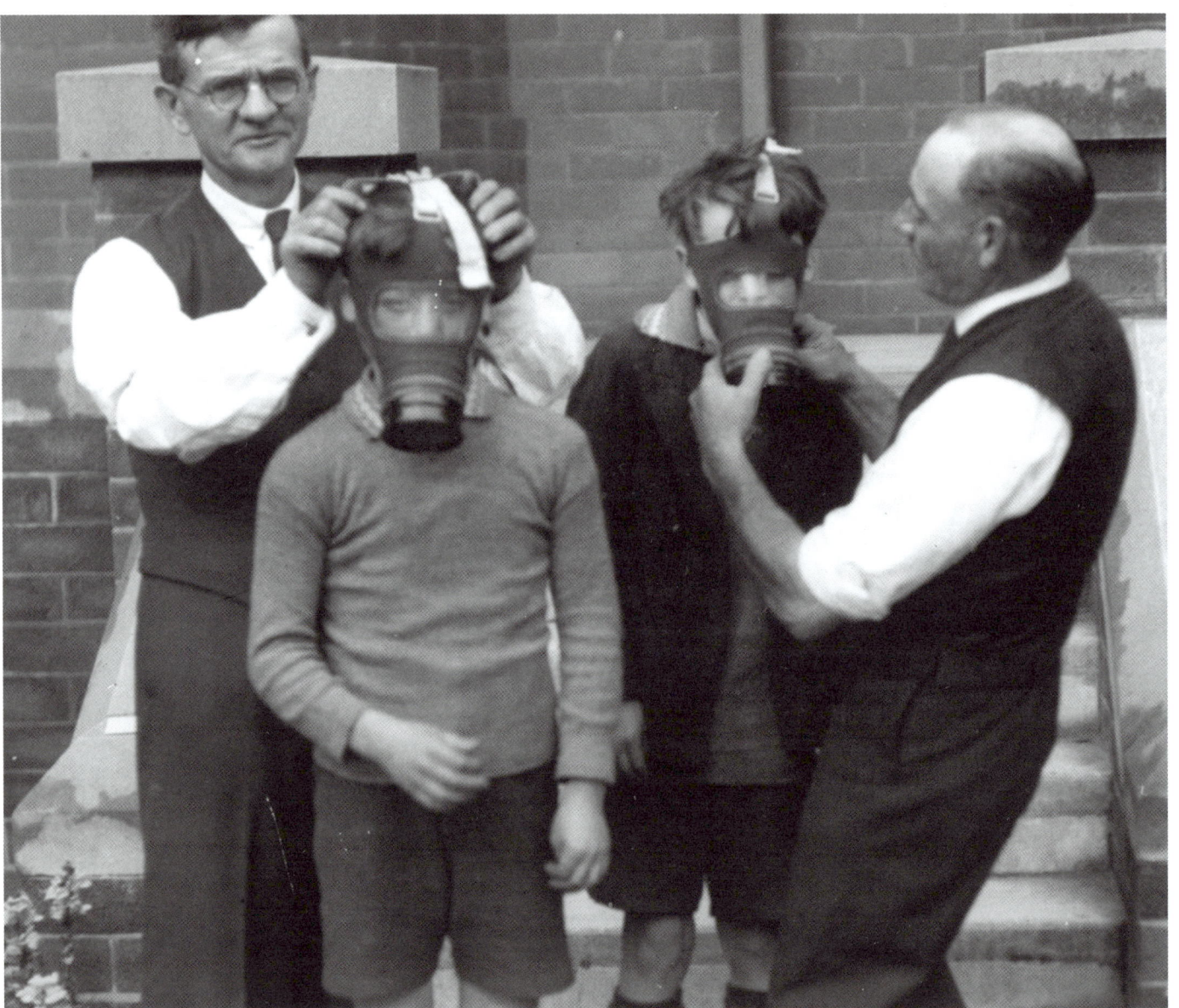

Fitting boys with gas masks, Newcastle 1939

People who lived through the war years will recognise the Air Raid Precautions cigarette cards first produced in 1938 but few realise they were made at the factory of W. D. and H. O. Wills on Coast Road, Newcastle

In September 1935 Prime Minister Stanley Baldwin issued a circular entitled Air Raid Precautions (ARP) that invited local authorities to set up working committees and undertake measures, such as the construction of public shelters, to protect the populace. In response to the circular, the City and County Council of Newcastle formed its first ARP committee. The first units of the Observer Corps on Tyneside were established the following year and Newcastle Council established an Air Raid Precautions Department with offices on Jesmond Dene Road, publishing its first manual, the Synopsis of Anti Gas Training, in 1937. The use of bombers by the Luftwaffe against civilian targets during the Spanish Civil War, especially the use of fire bombs, caused concerns over our preparedness to combat the fires that may be caused in this country in the event of another war with Germany. There was no RADAR to monitor aircraft over land at that time so the spotting, plotting and relaying of information about aircraft over Britain fell to the Observer Corps (OC). Because of the military sensitive natures of their duties, all OC volunteers were originally sworn in as Special Constables. In effect the OC volunteers served two masters: the police who maintained them and the military authorities for Air Defence.

The location of OC Posts was always dependant on their proximity to centres of habitation and telephone lines, allowing them to phone through reports to the plotting centre and thus creating a warning system to alert the RAF about the approach of enemy bombers. Most observers provided their own binoculars and were supplied with a post plotting instrument. Northumberland and Durham became Observer Corps Group 30, with Captain E.G. Jones as Controller with Head Special Constable Lancelot Telford in charge of the Newcastle corps.

Calls were also made from the fire brigade associations and Institution of Fire Engineers for an expansion of the fire force and the establishment of reserves of equipment to stand ready in the event of war. As a result, an Act of Parliament authorised the creation of a voluntary fire service and the Auxiliary Fire Service was founded as part of the Air Raid Precautions (ARP) organisation in January 1938. In March 1938 Home Secretary Sir Samuel Hoare made a radio appeal for a million volunteers for ARP work. From that time onwards a small government staff based in Newcastle, working under a Senior Regional Officer, began to advance the creation of the ARP scheme in the region and actively recruit and train the volunteers to staff it. Both men and women could train in a variety of roles in ARP and recruitment was certainly spurred on by the Munich Crisis of 1938, when the ARP and community volunteers worked together to assemble and distribute thousands of gas masks to the public.

When the National Service booklet that explained the roles of military and civilian services recruiting for volunteers was sent to every household in January 1939 recruitment stepped up and was further encouraged by appeals for volunteers in the national and local media. Within days of the issue of the booklet the Newcastle Observer Corps was fully recruited at its Kenton Post and a long waiting list had been drawn up.

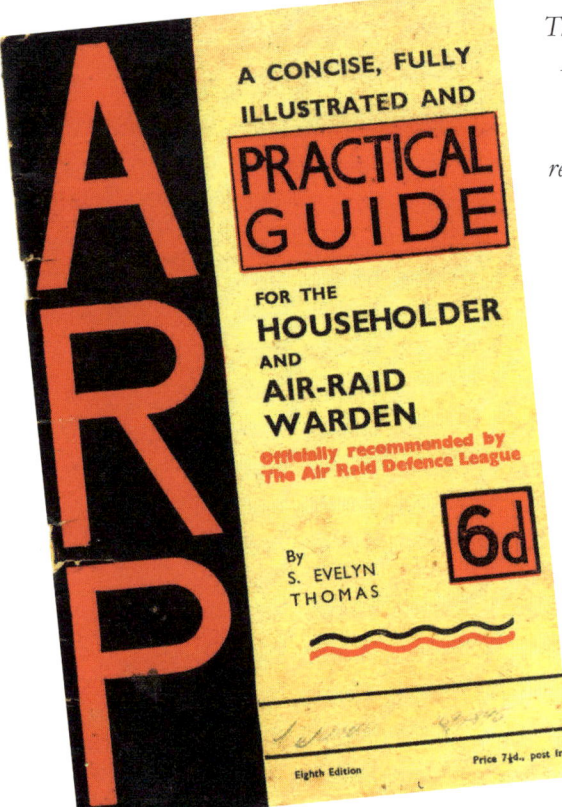

The ARP Practical Guide, essential reading in 1939

Other wartime organisations attracted volunteers by publishing newspaper appeals for roles like ambulance drivers, first aid parties and the auxiliary fire service.

Public demonstrations of the work of the ARP services always drew large crowds and attracted more volunteers. At the time National Service was published Newcastle had 1,100 Auxiliary Firemen but recruitment was still open for more and many factories and works that did not previously have their own fire brigade were inspired to establish Auxiliary Fire Service (AFS) units. Each AFS unit was issued with Coventry Victor, Coventry Climax or Sigmund trailer pumps, the latter built at the Sigmund Pumps Works on the Team Valley Estate. All of these pumps could be towed by civilian vehicles such as a taxi. Many AFS units raised by local businesses designated and even fully converted one of their

ARP Rescue squad members wearing gas masks and gas proof suits during an exercise staged outside the Newcastle Golf Club building on Claremont Road, Newcastle, February 1939

company's lorries specifically for AFS duties to carry both crews and additional rescue equipment such as ladders, ropes and foam branches.

A display was staged by the transport members of 'A' Division, Newcastle ARP and AFS on the morning of 29 January 1939. A column of eighteen cars, with full uniformed crew, ranging from small 8hp vehicles to massive saloons, each drawing small trailer pumps, toured the city, drawing large crowds to see the pumps in action on the Quayside. Meanwhile, in Gosforth *'the sirens sounded the air raid warning and soon wardens in their white arm bands could be seen patrolling the streets to see that the public were under cover before raiders came. An oily substance on the roadway at Grange Park indicated the presence of mustard gas calling to the services of a Decontamination Squad and two large fires and a number of small ones were extinguished by Auxiliary Fire patrols armed with stirrup pumps and buckets of water. Trained AFS teams were soon assisting extant fire brigades on 'shouts' to fires and were regularly praised for their good work'.*

The AFS soon recruited more women to fill roles as drivers, despatch riders and canteen workers. Teenage boys, often recruited enblock from local Boys' Brigade units or Boy Scout patrols were taken on as AFS Messengers who, riding their bicycles, would assist in running messages, ensuring equipment and personnel were deployed and directed to where they were needed, especially when communications broke down during air raids.

Firefighting during a black-out exercise near St Andrew's Church, Newcastle, May 1939

Over the first week in May 1939 posters and notices were displayed on public service vehicles and street standards, asking the public to ensure their houses were properly prepared for the black-out and requesting people's co-operation in the first large-scale blackout exercise over Tyneside. This was held between 1.00am and 3.00am on Sunday 5 May 1939, during which time two mock air raids were conducted and thirty-three 'bombs' fell on Newcastle, fourteen of which would, as part of the exercise, fall across the city and cause fires. The remainder concentrated on the central area. The idea was to test the response time for the various ARP services and how they would perform during blackout conditions. Spotter planes from the RAF were scheduled to fly over the city to observe and report on the efficiency of the blackout. More than eighty square miles from Sunderland to Blyth were 'Blacked out' and over 30,000 ARP volunteers took part. Unfortunately, the RAF spotter planes were prevented from flying on account of fog but North East Regional Civil Commissioner, Sir Arthur Lambert, and his team made a tour of the towns during the exercise. The exercise went well but he did not welcome onlookers who seemed to make a joke of it nor those who drove in to watch proceedings and turned their car headlights on for a better look!

Parades and public demonstrations by ARP services were always well supported and good for recruitment. On 25 May 1939 members of the Wallsend ARP services gathered for their National Service parade. Led by the band of Swan, Hunter and Wigram Richardson Wallsend Shipyard Prize Band, the 800 members of the AFS, St John Ambulance and Air Raid Wardens marched. An AFS Fire Engine and the ARP demolition parties mounted on lorries added to the spectacle as they paraded through Willington Quay and Wallsend to the Borough Field, passing crowds that were six people deep in places.

A Newcastle Centre for the Women's Voluntary Services for Civil Defence was opened on 17 June 1939 at 136 Northumberland Street in premises loaned to them by the Newcastle National Service Committee. By July 1939 the preparations for a war emergency in Newcastle were in full flow. The ARP services required 3,180 wardens, 1,492 auxiliary firemen, 648 communications staff and 628 Special Constables.

At the meeting of the Newcastle Watch (ARP) Committee, the City Engineer, Mr P. Parr, reported that 220,000 people would need domestic shelter in the city and of these 160,000 were entitled to free shelters. Public shelters would be needed for 33,000. Garden shelters would protect 67,000, trenches for 4,500 in parks and streets were already built with more under construction that would provide shelter for a further 3,500. A scheme to convert basements into shelters was planned to offer 6,000 more spaces. Public shelters were also created at Ouseburn Culvert, Victoria Tunnel and Benwell Drift, which would bring the total number of spaces providing shelter in the city to 95,500. Tenders were also approved for the construction of an experimental trench shelter for 100 people in Sycamore Street.

On the day Hitler invaded Poland (25 August) notices were posted around Newcastle to make the public aware of the air raid warning sounds and what they signified: Warning of Impending Raid: Fluctuating or 'warbling' signal of varying pitch, or succession of intermittent blasts by hooters or sirens. These may be supplemented by sharp blasts on police whistles

Raiders passed: A continuous blast on police whistles

If poison gas has been used: Warning by hand rattles.

Gas danger passed: Ringing of hand bells

In the evening of 25 August 7,000 Newcastle ARP workers were called out in a drill to test the speed of their response. The *Newcastle Mercury* picks up the story: *"Every type of civilian defence worker and vehicle answered the call. Ambulances, private cars labelled for various duties, lorries towing trailer pumps and other lorries ready to transport decontamination and rescue squads were drawn up outside the various ARP depots and police stations in the city. Hand-picked employees of the Newcastle and Gateshead Gas Company Lighting Department were charged with ensuring the city would be blacked out at a moment's notice. Each man was given a certain area to cover, extinguishing street lamps, and mobile towers were ready for putting out elevated lights. Fortunately electric lighting could be put out across the city via central switches."*

By the time war broke out on 3 September 1939 there were 84 points in the city where ambulances were stationed and ready for immediate action, as were 75 rescue and demolition gangs. Full-time auxiliary firemen worked rotas to provide nearly 650 crewmen at any time of the day in the city. During the 'Phoney War,' between late September 1939 and early May 1940, the AFS was rarely needed and took the brunt of criticism levelled at the ARP services 'as a waste of money and manpower'. Its male members were often stigmatised as 'army dodgers.' As a result, combined with an increasingly grave situation emerging in France, significant numbers of the AFS began to resign and join other emergency organizations and military services. The Government was forced to step in with emergency legislation that 'froze' all firemen in the service. However, when the blitz began on London and as raids began to become more frequent on Tyneside nobody was left in any doubt of the value of auxiliary firemen.

From May 1940 air raid alert siren warnings became a regular feature of life for many people in urban areas. However, frequently no enemy aircraft passed over and valuable time was being wasted. It had a serious impact on essential war industries in Newcastle and Tyneside so roof-top spotters were posted on local factories allowing workers to continue to work after the siren sounded, only taking to their shelters when their local warning siren was sounded for a second time if enemy aircraft were directly approaching.

One of the first to be decorated for civilian gallantry with a George Medal was an Air Raid Warden from the North East. Patrick 'Pat' King of Shiremoor, a Great War veteran, who worked as a guard on the private railway of the Backworth Coal Company. Mr King had made it part of his duties to ensure Miss Hannah Wilson, who was blind, got to her shelter safely when the air raid sirens sounded. On 26 August 1940 a bomb dropped on her house before he was able to get there but Pat fought through the debris to get to her, even though a girder struck his head. When news of his award was announced Miss Wilson commented: *'I owe my life to him and nobody is more pleased than I that he has got his medal.'* Pat modestly said *'All I did was my best until the rest of the lads came along and then we got things cleared up.*

There were a variety of local and national organisations and schemes to help the victims of air raids. The first formed to supply clothing and comforts in Newcastle was the Ladies' Committee of Newcastle General War Hospital formed early in 1940. It was rapidly followed

A concrete air raid shelter under construction at Saville Place, Newcastle, September 1939

Drivers and Crew, Newburn ARP Ambulance Depot, 1941
Below: *St John Ambulance and Civil Nursing Reserve staff of First Aid Post, No. 6, Chillingham Road, Newcastle, 1942*

The Auxiliary Firemen staff members of Northern Coachbuilders, Newcastle 1941

by others that same year, notably the National Laundry Service founded by Sunderland launderer Mr. H. Lumsdon Taylor. Under the scheme laundries became places where old clothes could be donated, washed and cleaned and then distributed via civilian clothing depots run by the Women's Voluntary Service (WVS) and the Northumberland and Durham War Needs Fund. In the first three weeks some 3,000 garments were donated. The scheme soon took off and was widely adopted by members of the Institution of British Launderers.

By late 1940 there had been talk of the 'Battle of Britain' being won but Hitler had not finished his bombing campaign. Bombs had dropped in many locations other than London and the authorities were alive to the fact that having failed to break London there was a very good chance that enemy strategy would change and future attacks on Britain would be against other cities.

Each and every one of the incendiary bombs that rained down in their hundreds and thousands from enemy bombers could start a fire and the best way to deal with a fire was to extinguish it before it took hold and became a blaze. To deal with this menace, many of the area's historic buildings, factories and department stores had already started their own fire parties armed with sand, stirrup pumps and buckets but many more would be needed. The first national Fire Watchers Order was issued in September 1940 but it only required parties of fire watchers to be provided for factories where over thirty people were employed, at warehouses and timber yards and was extended to historic buildings, cathedrals and buildings of national importance.

In January 1941 a national Fire Watchers scheme was introduced that meant far more areas would have to have a fire watcher present twenty-four hours a day. Councillor W T Calerwood, Commandant of Newcastle AFS appealed for people not to wait until

Auxiliary Firemen and their trailer pump, Newcastle 1940

government legislation demanded action but to organise themselves into fire watching parties through the wardens of the districts in which they resided as soon as possible. Men, women and even people under sixteen could all participate. Calerwood suggested that through small weekly contributions from each householder street squads could soon be able to purchase ladders, scoops for fire bombs, stirrup pumps, helmets, first aid kits and other equipment. In conjunction with Councillor Calerwood's appeal, published in the Evening Chronicle, Mr G W Wilkinson, Secretary of the Barras Bridge Fire Watchers, described their scheme, which had four full-time Fire Watchers covering property from College Road to Eldon Place that had started on 31 December 1940.

Training for the new fire watchers would be provided by local air raid wardens of AFS units. The special correspondent of the *Newcastle Journal*, in a feature entitled Women May Join Fire Watchers, took pains to point out:

"Women are to be welcomed as fire watchers and it is possible that in business areas many women will be employed on this work ... It is calculated that an ordinary intelligent man or woman can learn to deal with fire bombs in half an hour."

During the summer of 1941, Supplementary Fire Parties were created on many streets to provide a rapid response unit to extinguish small fires caused by incendiary bombs. There was, however, little or no

in Newcastle in April 1941 was warmly welcomed by the city. Otherwise known as the 'Food Flying Squad,' the 100 mobile canteens had been presented to the nation by the USA. The fleet was the property of the Ministry of Food but worked under the control of the Regional Commissioner. Staffed by volunteers from the WVS, the canteens were deployed to provide for people in immediate need of food and nourishment anywhere in the northern region.

One destructive force of nature struck in Newcastle where the enemy bombs failed. On 25 July 1941 lighting hit the head of the statue of Earl Grey that has stood on a 130ft column since 1838. The head was shattered by the strike, sending fragments showering down to the street below. Fortunately no one was hurt, but the falling masonry smashed the big plate glass window of the Monument Hotel at the top of Grainger Street and

national co-ordination of the scheme and it was only in August 1941 that the national Fire Guard Organisation was established and Street Fire Parties were reorganised to become Fire Guards.

As the blitz spread across Britain's cities even more organisations came into being to help those in need. Sterling work was already being done by the mobile canteens of the YMCA, Salvation Army and WVS but there was always a need for more to lighten the load. The arrival of the Queen's Messenger's Food Convoys

Thousands of of the new style 'Zuckerman' helmets ready to issue to the new fire watchers, Newcastle, March 1941.

Methods of dealing with firebombs from an instructional manual 1941

TWO METHODS OF FIGHTING INCENDIARY BOMBS.
Note.—Gas-masks should not be used unless gas is present.

tramway and trolleybus overhead lines were damaged. As many pieces as possible of the statue were collected up and preserved with a view to repairing the statue. In 1947 sculptor Roger Hedley carved a new head based on the original fragments and the good Earl was restored to gaze out across the city again.

Newcastle and Tyneside sent numerous crews of firemen and appliances to help London and other blitzed cities but a problem soon emerged because the equipment used by the different brigades was often incompatible. Brigades had different rules and regulations and issues arose over who was in control. It was clear all fire brigades and AFS units should be unified and, as a result, all local fire authorities were taken over by the National Fire Service (NFS) in August 1941. Newcastle's first 'Firewoman' appointed under the NFS was Miss Marjorie Vickers of Gateshead, a former millinery showroom assistant, who began duty at Regional Fire Service Headquarters on 1 September 1941.

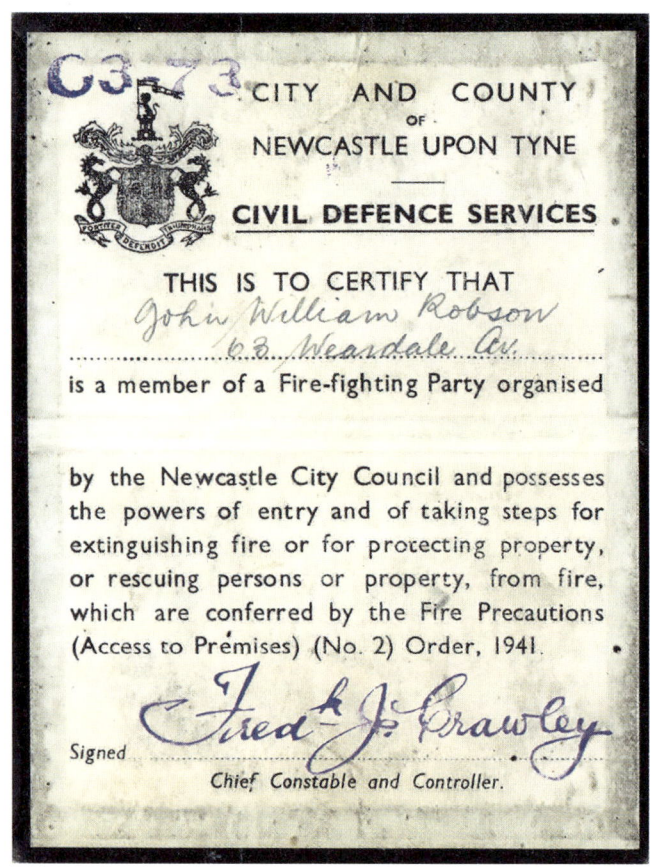

Firewatcher 'warrant' card issued by the City and County Council of Newcastle, 1941.

The new NFS also set out standardized equipment guidelines and created the first national training manual The National Fire Service Drill Book that clearly outlined the new rank structure, fire force locations, foot and appliance drills and words of command. The new standard methods were taught at training schools established in each fire force area. The NFS reached its height in 1942 when there were 100,000 full-time firemen, from a membership of 370,000 personnel, including 80,000 women on its establishment.

The Queen's Messengers Food Convoy and WVS staff, Newcastle April 1941.

The ARP Services had changed their name to Civil Defence (CD) in 1941, this was also a rebranding as they adopted smarter blue battledress uniforms and standardised ranks, badges and insignia. The men and women of the CD and NFS were never idle, they would often have to clean and maintain their vehicles after responding to a call, the women workers are well remembered for helping in this process and for their assistance in cleaning and drying the uniforms as well as supplying food and countless cups of tea (as did many other home front organizations from their mobile canteens). Male and female members of the NFS took part in daily keep fit regimes to maintain their efficiency throughout the war. In quiet periods many of them even undertook voluntary manufacturing work for the war effort in improvised workshops in or adjacent to their fire stations.

As the Allies obtained air superiority, full street lighting was gradually restored to most North-East towns from September 1944. The Air Raid Precaution organisation, then known as Civil Defence, was gradually wound down from its huge wartime membership numbers. In

Members of Newcastle Civil Defence Rescue Service, Henderson Hall, Newcastle, August 1942

March 1945 Sir Arthur Lambert, Regional Commissioner, sent a farewell message to all personnel in the Northern (No 1) Region and the official 'stand down' for all volunteers in the Civil Defence, Royal Observer Corps and National Fire Service took effect from 2 May 1945.

The Fire Services Act became law on 31 July 1947, which meant the NFS was unscrambled with effect from 1 April 1948 and the administration of fire brigades was handed over to counties and boroughs again. The Civil Defence Committee also continued to meet after the war to see out the disposal of their surplus vehicles and equipment, many of the 6,578 communal surface shelters in Newcastle were demolished, Anderson and Morrison shelters were collected in and sold for scrap as were the thousands of steel helmets that were sold at £5 per ton.

Above: Members of a Newcastle Civil Defence First Aid Party, 1941. Left: Civil Defence Ambulance Drivers, Heaton Park Road Depot, 1941

Above: Youth Branch British Red Cross Society Officers and members, North Heaton, 1944.
Right: Members of Newcastle Civil Defence Wardens Service, Cragside November 1944

AIR RAIDS

Damage from an air raid at Wallsend, 25 April, 1941

The first air raid warning siren of the war was sounded the day war broke out but no aircraft came. In fact between the outbreak of war in September 1939 and May 1940 the air offensive raids against Britain had been restricted to a mine laying mission in the waters around our country rather than the 'knock out blow' many feared, nor was there any offensive against military or civilian targets on British soil. Sadly, however, that did not mean there were no casualties. With blackouts enforced across the country, street lights were turned off and there was a huge increase in accidents caused by poor visibility on the darkened streets. Consequently kerbs, corners of buildings, street door frames, car running boards and bumpers and street obstacles such as trees, lamp posts and bollards had white bands painted on them and people had to think carefully about how they could be seen in the blackout by wearing white coats, arm bands or head scarves or carrying newspapers or white brollies.

Even those inspecting premises for blackout compliance faced dangers as they traversed unfamiliar buildings, even when escorted. One notable tragedy occurred in October 1939 when Newcastle Fire Brigade Superintendent Norman Murray was inspecting the Tatler News Cinema on Northumberland Street. After checking the various fire and emergency lighting appliances in the cinema, the manager demonstrated the panic bolts on the fire exit door in the projection room and, before he had a chance to warn him, Superintendent Murray walked past him into darkness and fell through the small aperture in the fire escape platform outside the door. Sustaining a fractured skull, the fire chief was taken to the Royal Victoria Infirmary where he died the following day.

The first name to be listed on the Commonwealth War Graves Commission Civilian War Dead Roll of Honour for the North East is also a fireman. Auxiliary Fireman Charles Rutherford (45) of Hedley Street, Gosforth died when the Gosforth Fire Engine he was travelling in overturned while on its way to attend to a farm fire at Shotton on 20 December 1939.

It would not be until 3 February 1940 that the first enemy aircraft, a Heinkel IIIH, was brought down on English soil by Flight Lieutenant Peter Townsend flying a Hurricane from 43 Squadron, Acklington. The enemy aircraft had been attacking a ship off Whitby, Yorkshire when it was intercepted by Townsend and, after a short burst from his machine guns, it was sent down with a trail of smoke behind it and crash landed at Bannial Flat Farm, Whitby.

Towns and cities in the North East suffered their first bombs on 25 May 1940 when Middlesborough was the first industrial town to be hit. On 6 June 1940 the first civilian lives were lost in the North East when the pilot of a Bristol Beaufighter, returning from a raid on Ghent, was dazzled by searchlights as he crossed the coast at Blyth. Flying low to avoid them, he hit barrage balloon cables. Two crew managed to bail out but the

The burnt out shell of the old Spillers warehouse, Newcastle after the first raid on the city, 2 July 1940

stricken aircraft fell on 77 Fifth Row, Ashington, claiming the lives of Henry (52) and Eleanor Cox (49). Their daughter Gladys (18) was taken to hospital where she died of her wounds. The first member of the Air Raid Precautions organisation to be killed during an enemy air raid was Warden John Punton (54) of West

Hartlepool, who was killed during the raid on the town on 20 June 1940.

There were hundreds of alerts, raids and incidents over Newcastle and Tyneside during the war. The following accounts describe some of the most significant.

The first bombs fell on Newcastle during a daylight raid at approximately 5.30pm on Tuesday 2 July 1940. In what was believed to have been an attempt to bomb the High Level Bridge, a single Dornier flew over Blaydon, brought down a barrage balloon and, sweeping towards the bridge, dropped a high explosive bomb that fell on the old Spiller's Mill warehouse where John Kelly (28) was killed while he was in the process of locking up and five others were injured. Another bomb fell into the Tyne a few feet from the bridge and one fell on Hawthorn Leslie's engineering works on Forth Street. A number of shops and buildings on nearby roads also had their windows blown out by the bomb blast. The raider flew on to Jarrow where he ditched three bombs on the streets, reducing a number of buildings to rubble, killing 14 people and injuring 120.

On the night of 28-29 July 1940 enemy bombers returned to Newcastle and dropped 25 high explosive bombs almost in a straight line across the city. In the Heaton area five houses were shattered, another bomb crashed through the roof into the dining hall at Heaton Secondary School, others fell in the quadrangle and wrecked the nearby caretaker's house. The raid killed three people including a woman who was trying to warn her neighbours, and injured a number others. The next raid came on 11 August 1940 and was part of a series called 'rumour raids'. About 100 firebombs fell on the city starting 18 small fires that were all extinguished by fire parties and ARP workers with no loss of life.

On 15 August 1940 the Luftwaffe attempted its first mass daylight raid on the North East. The following vivid first-hand account of the 'Air Battle of Tyneside' was written by James Brunskill for the Newcastle Victory Celebrations souvenir programme in 1946:

'On that fateful summer day of 15 August 1940 between 180 and 200 German bombers tried to smash our industrial areas. Lunch-hour crowds hurried to shelter as waves of enemy planes droned ominously nearer until their engines sounded like the roar of thunder and only the skill and courage of the RAF pilots and accurate AA fire saved Newcastle and other places from death and destruction. The attacking force was a mixed formation of Heinkel and Junkers bombers escorted by 36 Messerschmitt 110 fighters flying astern and above them. Into the Luftwaffe formations tore our defiant Spitfire and Hurricane fighters weaving, spiralling and diving, their machine guns spitting death and they speedily converted a desperate and determined attack into what for the enemy was a costly and ghastly failure. Seventy-five German planes were destroyed or crippled within as many minutes, while many more would probably never reach their base. The 'raiders past' sounded and citizens emerged from their underground shelters into the brilliant sunshine. Womenfolk resumed their shopping and men returned to their offices ... the life of Newcastle went on as before.'

This action was undoubtedly the most significant day for the North East during the Battle of Britain. In his *Air War Over the North East* retrospective articles in the *Evening Chronicle* in 1942, S. E. Sterck wrote:

'It was a glorious victory and one that was destined to mark the turn in aerial supremacy. Skill and daring. British courage at its apex the spirit of Nelson and Drake reincarnated in the twentieth century men of the air.'

The Luftwaffe would refer to this day as 'Black Thursday' and never again sent such numbers against the North East.

The mass bomber formations over Tyneside stopped for a while but there were a few 'sneak' or 'tip and run'

Above: Damage at Whitley Bay after the air raid of 9/10 April 1941. Right: Damage at North Shields after the air raid of 9/10 April 1941

raids conducted by bombers that flew low over the sea to avoid detection during the rest of August. On 25 August 1940 enemy raiders dropped four bombs on and near the Neptune Shipyard at Walker; unlike other areas in the North East on that night there were no casualties. Matters took a turn for the worse, however, when an enemy plane roared in from the sea over Monkseaton and Whitley Bay on the night of 28-29 August, dropping three bombs which wrecked three churches, a hall and a school, killed one and injured several other people.

The enemy raiders returned on the night of 3-4 September and dropped a high explosive bomb on Jenifer Grove and caused major damage to Cloverdale Gardens, North Heaton, wrecking three houses and damaging 30 more with its blast. One woman was killed by a shell splinter and five people were injured, including one man who was blown out of his bedroom window to the bottom of his garden. Far worse would come in the raids of the following year that would be remembered locally as 'the ordeal of 1941.'

The enemy raiders returned to Tyneside with a vengeance on the night of 15-16 February 1941. Waves of bombers came over, the anti-aircraft guns opened

Damage at Jarrow after the air raid of 9/10 April 1941

up and there was constant aerial activity punctuated by the sound of bombs exploding. In Northumberland many of the shop windows in Blyth town centre were shattered. Bedlington and North Blyth received two high explosive bombs, severely damaging blocks of houses. They also suffered a shower of incendiaries but thanks to the prompt actions of the volunteer firewatchers, who extinguished many of the bombs, damage was limited to three private residences and the Co-op. Hundreds of people had to be evacuated from Tynemouth because of the number of delayed action bombs that had been dropped.

One of the heaviest raids inflicted on Northumberland during the entire war occurred on the night of 9-10 April 1941 when 116 enemy aircraft dropped an estimated 152 tonnes of high explosive (HE) bombs and thousands of incendiaries on docks, dock yards and industries along the Tyne from Newcastle to Tynemouth. One of the fires started in a timber yard and grew to a mile-long blaze attended by fire appliances from Newburn, Gosforth and Blyth. Hundreds of smaller fires had been started but were swiftly dealt with by well-prepared ARP wardens, AFS and householders. Incendiaries rained down on Newcastle and firewatchers took these on with aplomb but Tynemouth seemed to receive the brunt of HE bombs, which damaged many shops and homes across the Borough.

Some of the incendiaries fell on and around the three gas holders of the Newcastle and Gateshead Gas Co. works at Tynemouth, some even penetrated the metal tops and fell into the coal gas below. Fortunately there was no oxygen in the holders so the bombs failed to ignite, but the holes hissing out the gas had to be quickly filled. The men from the works came running to see what they could do, fearing the worst for the town if they all 'went up'. In retrospect they were all amazed that when the HE bombs started falling and exploding

Guildford Place with Cheltenham Terrace in the background, Heaton after the air raid of 25 April 1941

around them, throwing up grit, stones and mud none of them had a direct hit on one of the gas holders. None of them seemed to be thinking of their personal safety while this was going on - their over-riding concern was to make those gas holders safe again. Yard Foreman Joseph Callaghan climbed up the holders and began sealing the holes as best he could until he was overcome by fumes. Others helped too. Gas Works Yard Manager George Duncan was helping keep everyone calm and dealing with the incendiaries with his daughter Lorna (20), who scaled a 60ft-high gas holder, dressed only in a dressing gown, carrying up a wire handled bucket of clay to plug the holes. A total of 35 people lost their lives in this raid, but the death toll could have been far worse if it had not been for the prompt, brave actions of those at the gasworks. In recognition of their actions Lorna Duncan received a commendation, her father was presented with an MBE and Yard Foreman Joseph Callaghan was decorated with the George Medal.

Above The damage inflicted on Wilkinson's Lemonade Factory on the corner of Kings Street and George Street, Tynemouth, after the raid of 3/4 May 1941 and its the basement shelter that suffered a collapse and 107 people lost their lives.

Left: Damage at Wallsend after the air raid of 25 April 1941.
Above: Damage near the railway junction at Blyth after the air raid of 25 April 1941

On the dark, still night of 25 April 1941 enemy aircraft bombed the Heaton, Byker, Jesmond and Quayside areas of Newcastle. No siren had sounded before nine high explosive bombs fell on Shields Road, Jesmond Vale, Heaton Park, Sutherland Park and Grace Street, incendiaries clattered onto Heaton Road and a parachute mine drifted down silently and exploded in Guildford Place blast-damaging Cheltenham Terrace. Resident Robert Walsh recalled the night; he had gone up the road to Meadowfield Social Club to have a drink and pay his sick fund money *'when suddenly there was this almighty bang. It was a thudding sort of noise, as though something was bouncing. It was so close, it was like someone had discharged a rifle an inch from your ear.'* Fearing the bomb had got his home, his wife and family, he went running back to find his house had been badly damaged. His wife was injured but she and the children were all alive.

The houses beside them, however, had been shattered and others reduced to a sickening mass of rubble and broken domestic effects. As the fire and rescue crews arrived, they could see they had an immense task ahead of them. One memory that lingered was the old lady who was wandering around with her hands covering her mouth. A member of the rescue crew went to ask if she was OK and was relieved to learn that she had managed to escape from the wreckage of her home but had not had a chance to find her false teeth. Not everyone was so fortunate; 35 people were killed at Guildford Place, among them six members of the Angus family, Joan Hagon and her three children, Francis and Ethel Park and their daughter Mavis, Joseph Dixon Reed, his wife Alice and their nine-week old grandson Joseph Lancelot Reed. At nearby Cheltenham Terrace four members of the Robson family also lost their lives as did Air Raid Wardens Thomas and William Shaw. It took five days for the rescue parties to pick through the rubble before everyone could be accounted for. All told, 47 people lost their lives as a result of the raid on Heaton. Numerous houses were also damaged at Wallsend, where a further 17 people lost their lives. HE and incendiaries were dropped on Blyth, damaging houses, killing two people, seriously injuring 10 and slightly injuring 63. A large public shelter that stood nearby was also seriously damaged in the bomb blast. Home Guardsman George Evans and Special Constable Jack Furness were blown down the steps. On recovering they discovered the entrance was starting to collapse and, bracing their backs to the walls, they held them as long as they could so most of the people managed to get out. The men eventually had to let go. The four people who were left inside were later rescued uninjured from the rubble.

Less than a month later a raid took place on the North East during which a tragedy occurred of such magnitude that when many other events from the war have been forgotten its story has been handed down by successive generations of locals to the present day. Shortly before midnight on the night of 3 May 1941 a single enemy raider was detected, the sirens wailed their warning and people of North Shields took cover in their air raid shelters. One bomb proved to be a dud but another made a direct hit on Wilkinson's mineral water and soda manufacturers, known locally as 'the lemonade factory,' on the corner of King Street and George Street. The building and its machinery collapsed into the public air raid shelter beneath it where 103 people were sheltering.

Many were killed instantly and, despite the heroic and tireless efforts of the Special Constables and ARP workers who were first on the scene, the final death toll stood at 107 men, women and children. A total of 43 children under the age of 16 died in the tragedy. Some families suffered more than one loss; Alfred and Henrietta Chater and their four children were all killed, as were Martha Hall and her five children and Doreen Kay with her four sons. ARP Rescue Party leaders Clarence Burdis and George Newstead were both

Policemen and soldiers survey the wreckage of Rudolf Hess' (left) crashed Messerschmitt at Eaglesham

awarded George Medals and First Aid Party member Norman Darling Black received a British Empire Medal for their gallantry at the scene. Sadly the Shelter Marshal, Mrs Ellen Lee, who was herself badly burned but carried on helping the injured and personally created an escape route for a number of people to get out, was never officially recognised for her deeds and remains the unsung heroine of the night. The direct hit on Wilkinson's caused the worst loss of life from a single bomb on Tyneside during the war.

At 10.25 on 10 May 1941, a lone enemy fighter aircraft was spotted crossing the Northumberland coastline by the Royal Observer Corps Post at Embleton and was reported to 30 Group ROC Operations Centre at

Durham. A further report was received a few minutes later from the ROC Post at Chatton, where Head Observer Mr GW Green identified the aircraft as a Messerschmitt Bf110. The aircraft was then plotted by further posts as it headed over the border into Scotland. Sergeant Maurice Pocock of 72 Squadron, RAF Acklington was sent up in his Spitfire to intercept the enemy aircraft but the Messerschmitt went into a steep dive and disappeared in the darkness. The Messerschmitt's pilot bailed out and landed in a field near Eaglesham, East Renfrewshire where he was soon picked up. Enemy aircraft and pilots bailing out over England were not uncommon but after giving his name as Alfred Horn this particular pilot's true identity was soon recognised - he was none other than Hitler's Deputy, Rudolf Hess! There has been conjecture over Hess's sanity and his motives for the flight ever since. It has been suggested Hess believed he was coming to discuss a peace deal to be brokered by the Duke of Hamilton, something the Duke strenuously denied. Arthur Askey had a hit with the comedy song *'Thanks for Dropping in Mr Hess.'*

On the brilliant moonlit night of 11-12 May 1941, raiders came for Newcastle again and dropped several HE bombs on Jesmond, one demolishing a house at the corner of Shortridge Terrace and Farquhar Street. Whickham, Middlesborough, Hartlepool, Darlington and Stockton also suffered that night.

Many of those who were kids in wartime remember playing among the debris on bomb sites although their parents would warn them not to play there, and with good reason as Irene Page (7) discovered on 31 May 1941. Irene, the daughter of Wansbeck Street coal dealer John Page, had been playing with friends on the bomb-damaged area in Back Tarset Street, Newcastle when she fell down a bomb crater that was about 30 inches in diameter but was 10ft deep. Little Irene was overcome by fumes that still lingered at the bottom of the crater. Boy Scout Ernest Smith rushed to help her and, taking hold of a rope, said 'Let me do it. I will tie the rope the Scout way' and he volunteered to be lowered down to rescue her but he too succumbed to the fumes. Off-duty Auxiliary Fireman John Tulip, Irene's uncle, tried next, followed by another AFS Fireman George Wanless but again both were overcome by the deadly fumes.

The police, fire brigade and ambulance were soon on the scene. Fireman Laurence 'Larry' Young, completely without protection against the fumes and fully aware that the previous attempts had proven fatal, with the assistance of Leading Fireman Bruce, descended into the crater. Bruce collapsed on account of the fumes and Fireman Young went to his aid, Young then returned to the crater but all he could do was recover the bodies. Fireman Larry Young was awarded the George Medal for his bravery, Leading Fireman Bruce recovered and was commended for his part in the rescue attempt, Auxiliary Fireman Wanless was awarded a posthumous commendation and the brave young Scout Ernest Smith, who gave his life to help a friend, was awarded a posthumous Boy Scouts Bronze Cross for heroism on 25 June 1941.

Another bright moonlit night on 1-2 September 1941 saw Newcastle subjected to a raid conducted by 25 long-range bombers that dropped 100 bombs across the city from Northumberland Road to Wallsend and as far north as Jesmond Dene Road. Shieldfield, Jesmond, St. Peters, Byker and Walker all suffered. A total of 49 people were killed, 71 seriously injured and over 1,000 left homeless. The most significant structure severely damaged in the raid was the New Bridge Street Goods Station at Manors' which received a direct hit from an oil bomb, quickly followed by two HE bombs. Tom Robson, the driver of a heavy railway truck, had finished his evening duty with the Home Guard and had just reached his home on Argyle Street when he saw the

flames from the station and ran to help. He recalled:
'I wanted to save as many Scammel trucks as I could so I dashed into the ground floor of the warehouse. The oil was falling from above like a sluggish waterfall of molten metal, splashing as it reached the floor and snaking out in small rivers of flame.'

Helped by checker Frank McKenzie, he managed to get a few away as the structure blazed and rumbled over their heads. Over 70 wagons full of food were rescued at great risk by volunteer railway workers at the goods station but the fire was spreading all the time, connecting with others started by the other bombs on the station. The warehouse blaze intensified, the structure began to shake and the front collapsed, making the rescue of more impossible.

The warehouse contained over 300 tons of food such as flour, margarine and sugar, which fuelled an inferno that shot pillars of flame 200ft skyward. The fire or its vivid red glow in the night sky could be seen from many areas of the city and many worried that it would act as a beacon to draw more bombs from other raiders. Houses in the area were evacuated but fortunately no other bombers came over during the next two days as fire crews struggled to extinguish the blaze. Always feeling he had simply done his bit, Tom Robson received a King's Commendation for his bravery.

The foggy night of 29-30 December 1941 saw 55 enemy aircraft target Tyneside. When over Newcastle they discharged a total of 10 high explosive bombs, which landed on High Heaton, Byker, Jesmond, Dudley and Newburn, four of them landed on Keys Gardens and the Matthew Bank area of Gosforth. Each bomb finding its mark on or so close to houses they inflicted severe blast damage, causing seven fatalities, ten people were seriously injured and ten more suffered minor injuries in that area alone. Among them was eight-year-old Newton Shipley whose legs were crushed by the falling debris of his home. When the rescue worker dug him out, he congratulated the lad on being so brave to which he replied *'Of course. Don't you know I'm a Wolf Cub.'* Newton had one leg amputated and would face a number of painful operations to have the other re-set a number of times. In 1950 he was awarded the Cornwell Badge for his high character, courage and endurance by the Boy Scout Association.

After the tragedy of Matthew Bank there were only three more alerts sounded in Newcastle, no more bombs were dropped but the fragments of Anti-Aircraft shells fired up by the guns to send the enemy raiders away fell back to the ground and damaged a number of houses. Between July 1940 and December 1941 nearly 400 people had been killed during air raids or as a result of enemy action on Tyneside. Between June 1940 and the last siren sounding in October 1944 Newcastle had 238 alerts and suffered 31 raids, an estimated 200 high explosive bombs and around 2,000 incendiaries had been dropped, as a result of which 142 people lost their lives, 177 were seriously injured and 403 suffered more minor injuries.

The smouldering ruins of New Bridge Street Goods Station at Manors, Newcastle, after the air raid of 1-2 September 1941

Keyes Gardens, Matthew Bank, Gosforth, after the air raid of 29-30 December 1941

THE MILITARY

Presentation of the original bass drum of the Tyneside Scottish, Jesmond, January 1940

Conscription for men was introduced from the outbreak of war and consequently the army, which consisted of almost one million men including Reserves in 1939 had expanded to three million men by 1945. Initially, the locally raised Regular Army and Territorial Army units would have been filled with men from Newcastle and Northumberland.

After the Dunkirk evacuation, new recruits outnumbered the pre-war regular soldiers that were left and the average soldier at the sharp end of the fighting was in fact a 'Citizen soldier' for the rest of the war. Many of them were conscripted from men aged between eighteen and forty-one. The average British infantryman tended to be in his mid-twenties and, as the war progressed and more and more men were conscripted, men of Newcastle and Tyneside ended up serving in a huge array of British Army regiments, the Royal Navy and the Royal Air Force.

The men from the North had a huge variety of educational backgrounds, affluent, poor and everything in-between, but what they did have in common was around sixteen weeks' training to be soldiers and no previous military or combat experience, a reputation for good comradeship and a fighting spirit second to none.

The British Expeditionary Force and Dunkirk

The troops of the BEF arrived in France and were greeted as heroes as they marched through towns and villages to take up their defensive positions beside the Maginot line. The troops dug in and then waited week after week, but no attack came. Through the bitterly cold winter of 1939-40 American newspapers began to talk of a 'Phoney War' and even British newspapers struggled to keep interest in a stagnant campaign that seemed very distant to the British public. As the old year drew to an end, newspapers ran stories of our lads celebrating Christmas on the front line and one of the most famous images was an official war photograph and the first to show British and French troops sharing a drink to celebrate New Year. The soldier chosen to represent British troops for the posed image was local man, Sapper George Stephenson (32), 26th Field Company, Royal Engineers of Percy Crescent, Percy Main. The picture captured something of the mood of the time, a timeless comradeship reminiscent of the Great War and so poignant as the soldiers faced a New Year not knowing what fate held for them. The photograph was reproduced in newspapers, magazines and other publications syndicated all over the world.

The whole situation changed on 9 May 1940 when Hitler unleashed his Blitzkrieg and the British forces were knocked onto their heels and sent reeling into a fighting retreat to the French coast and evacuation from the beaches of of Dunkirk. What is often forgotten is that the 51st (Highland) Division (including 26th Company Royal Engineers), reinforced by a number of other units including many lads from Newcastle, Northumberland and Tyneside, specifically: 23rd (Northumbrian) Infantry Division that had both 8th (Motorcycle) Battalion and 9th (Machine Gun) Battalions, Northumberland Fusiliers within it and 70th Infantry Brigade that comprised 10th and 11th

The front cover of The War Weekly, featuring Geordie soldier George Stephenson (centre) in the first official photograph of BEF soldiers with French soldiers, December 1939

Battalions, Durham Light Infantry and 1st Battalion, Tyneside Scottish were all part of Saar Force, which was assigned to the French Third Army. Saar Force remained in France after the main evacuation from Dunkirk.

Despite great plans for a counter offensive it never took place. As their stocks of ammunition ran out, a naval evacuation for these men proved impossible and the majority of them were either killed in action or taken prisoners of war when the Division surrendered at St Valery en Caux. The loss of life was heavy and among the dead was Sapper George Stephenson. In a letter to George's sister in Tynemouth, one of his comrades explained:

'Your brother noticed that one man had been hit badly. He crawled out to try and get him in when a big burst of trench mortar fire came within a few yards of him. He got back to his dugout and one of the boys bandaged him up as best he could and from there he was taken back behind the line and so we lost sight of him. That is all I can say but I feel sure that his act under such heavy fire will live for ever in the minds of us few men who were lucky enough to get home from France.'

George died on 9 June 1940; he is the only casualty to rest in the churchyard of Anneville-sur-Scie, just a few miles from Dieppe.

The Dunkirk evacuation saw numerous tragic incidents where friends and even family members were separated as they scrabbled to board the rescue vessels. Infantry soldier Private Walter Cann of Blaydon saw his nineteen year old son, also called Walter, left on the jetty as his ship pulled away. News reached his family that young Walter had been among those taken prisoner of war. The British Army would rebuild and return in 1944, but that would seem a long way off for the thousands of lads who spent the next five years in captivity.

The Royal Northumberland Fusiliers

The Northumberland Fusiliers had a long and distinguished history that could be traced back to 1653. In King George V's Silver Jubilee Honours of 1935 they were granted the 'Royal' prefix in recognition of their services in the First World War and those who served from then on could proudly say they were Royal Northumberland Fusiliers (RNF). The following year the RNF were one of four line infantry regiments selected for conversion to Divisional Machine Gun or

Two new recruit pals at Fenham Barracks, the Depot of the Royal Northumberland Fusiliers. Left: Royal Northumberland Fusiliers economy plastic badge issued during the war when metal for badges was deployed for munitions

Men from 4th Battalion, Royal Northumberland Fusiliers serving as part of Motor Cycle Reconnaissance Battalion, 50th (Northumbrian) Division, B.E.F making friends with the locals, 'somewhere in Belgium' 1940

Divisional Support Battalions. During the Second World War The Royal Northumberland Fusiliers expanded to a total of ten Battalions:

1st Battalion – North Africa (1939 - May 1943) Egypt, Syria, Palestine and Italy (May 1943 -1945).

2nd Battalion – Mobilised at Connaught Barracks, Dover, Machine Gun Battalion, 4th Division, B.E.F. France (1939 - Evacuated from Dunkirk June 1940). Invasion defence duties in Great Britain (June 1940 - 1943), North Africa and Italy (June 1943 - December 1944), Greece (December 1944 - May 1945).

4th Battalion – Motor Cycle Reconnaissance Battalion, 50th (Northumbrian) Division, B.E.F. France, evacuated from Dunkirk (1939 - June 1940). Invasion defence duties in Great Britain (June 1940 - June 1941), North Africa (August 1941- September 1942). Disbanded and as Battalion they formed 1, 2 and 3 Independent Machine-Gun Companies (1943- June 1944) Normandy and the Low Countries (June 1944 - September 1944). Advance into Germany (October 1944 - May 1945).

5th Battalion (TA) Searchlight Regiment serving on the Home Front through the Battle of Britain and beyond (1939 - May 1945) Norway (June 1945 - October 1945).

Battalion insignia of 4th Motor Cycle Battalion, Royal Northumberland Fusiliers T.A

Z Company, 9th Battalion, Royal Northumberland Fusiliers T.A. shortly before their departure for Singapore in October 1941

6th Battalion (TA) Duplicated and converted into two armoured units:

43rd (Northumberland) Battalion, Royal Tank Regiment – Home Defence, Motor Machine Gun Brigade and anti-invasion role (1939 - 1941). Part of Experimental Army Tank Division developing Hobart's 'Funnies' e.g. Flail Tanks, Buffaloes, Kangaroos and D.D. Tanks (1942 - 1944), India (1945).

43rd (Northumberland) Battalion, Royal Tank Regiment – Home Defence, Motor Machine Gun Brigade with anti-invasion role (1939 - 1941). Tank development work (1942 - 1944). France and Germany (August 1944 -1945).

7th Battalion Concentrated at Gosforth Park shortly after embodiment and training at Alton Hampshire (1939 - March 1940). Machine Gun Battalion 51st (Highland) Division, Saar Area, Maginot Line, France. Many killed or became Prisoners of War at St. Valery (March 1940 - June 1940). Battalion rebuilt and retrained then served on Home Defences (June 1940 - August 1943). Training for Operation Overlord (August 1943 - June 1944), France (June 1944 - Disbandment 20 September 1944).

8th Battalion Embodiment at Prudhoe and deployed to Home Front defences (1939 - April 1940). Motor Cycle Reconnaissance Battalion, 23rd (Northumbrian) Division France, Arras Defences (April 1940 - evacuated from Dunkirk and La Panne May 1940). Rebuilt and re-equipped and designation changed to 3rd Reconnaissance Regiment (N.F.) in spring 1941 (June 1940 - August 1943). Training for Operation Overlord (August 1943 - June 1944). Landed on D-Day, 6 June 1944 with 3rd Infantry Division, France and Low Countries (June 1944 - September 1944). The advance into Germany (October 1944 - May 1945).

Depot Band of the Royal Northumberland Fusiliers, Fenham Barracks, 1941

9th Battalion Embodied and sent as Machine Gun Battalion, 23rd (Northumbrian) Division, Monchy Breton France, (1939 - evacuated from Dunkirk May 1940). Embarked for Middle East with 18th Division (October 1941). Diverted to defend Singapore, landed 5 February 1942, fought in defence of Singapore until the surrender. Men of the battalion remained in Japanese captivity until September 1945.

10th (Home Defence) Battalion - Formed from 40 Group National Defence Company, redesignated 30th (H.D.) Battalion, Northumberland Fusiliers December 1941 (1939 - August 1943). Although styled 'Home Defence' the battalion was ordered to Algiers, North Africa (August 1943 - May 1944), Naples, Italy (1944), Garrison unit Malta (1944-45).

70th Battalion Formed at Gosforth and Benwell areas as a Young Soldiers battalion (1940). Headquarters remained at Gosforth with companies spread out as far as 50 miles from HQ on airfield defence work (1941-42). November 1942, battalion was at North Seaton Hall, Newbiggin when it converted to No. 98 Primary Training Centre and all surplus officers and men were transferred to other units.

The Depot - Remained at Fenham Barracks, which became a machine gun training centre until August 1941 when the MG training was centralised at Chester and small 'Depot Party' remained at Fenham. In turn this centre transferred to larger premises at Blacon Camp and the Regimental Depots moved there too. In December 1946 No.5 Primary Training Centre was formed at Fenham Barracks and the Regimental Depot was re-established there.

The Tyneside Scottish

The Tyneside Scottish raised not just one but a brigade of four battalions of volunteer soldiers for Kitchener's Army during the Great War; they had a distinguished war record but sadly were not carried on in peace time. So after the expansion of the Territorial Army was ordered but recruiting was lagging in the Durham area a number of people harked back to how rapidly the Tyneside Scottish battalions had recruited up to their quota and a suggestion was made in April 1939 to recruit the second line or 'duplicate' of 9th Battalion, Durham Light Infantry as Tyneside Scottish. On Thursday 11 May 1939 The War Office announced the Tyneside Scottish would be revived and designated 2/9th Battalion (Tyneside Scottish) Durham Light Infantry (TA). Soon retitled 12th Battalion (Tyneside Scottish), Durham Light Infantry (TA). The 9th Battalion's second-in-command, Gateshead solicitor Lieutenant Colonel Hugh Swinburne, became the Tyneside Scottish Battalion Commander with Captain E McClintock appointed as Adjutant.

Affiliation with a Highland Regiment was sought, and with the assent of The Black Watch the young battalion became part of the Regiment by Army Order 260/1939 on 20 December 1939 and on 1 January 1940 were retitled 1st Battalion, The Tyneside Scottish, The Black Watch (Royal Highland Regiment) and adopted the Black Watch Tartan and Red Hackle as well as a green lanyard to signify their DLI origin. *The Northern Echo* despatched a reporter to see the lads in training in late February:

'Operations began yesterday with a full parade and march past after which I saw routine exercises being carried out. These included signalling groups, bayonet practice, Bren, anti-tank gun and rifle training and a display by one of the battalion's ten carriers. These light armoured cars are used for transporting men and munitions up to advance positions across fire-swept country,

Badge of The Tyneside Scottish with The Black Watch backing worn during the Second World War.

which would be impassable to infantry, and their speed and mobility across rough country was astonishing to a layman'

The reporter also took pains to point out they were still looking for a few more men to bring the battalion up to full strength and listed the average daily menu for the battalion:

Breakfast: Tea, bread and butter, bacon and egg, tomato or beans, marmalade or jam.

Dinner: Roast beef or stew or tripe, vegetable and sweet.

Tea: Tea, bread, butter, cake, jam.

Supper: Tea, bread, margarine, salmon or soup or cheese.

The vexing question, as ever, was the kilt. The battalion, the Tyneside Scottish Committee and a party of Scots MPs were supporting the unit's representations to the Government to get permission to wear it. Major C W Oxley explained *'We appreciate that it is not the best kind of dress for modern war conditions but we do want it for walking out.'* A Pipe band was soon raised by kind donations but, just as in the Great War, only the pipers of the Tyneside Scottish would be permitted to wear kilts. During Church Parade at Jesmond Presbyterian Church on Sunday 7 January 1940, the bass drum of the original Tyneside Scottish of the Great War was presented to the battalion, a gift of the Newcastle Pipe Band, some eight of whose members formed the nucleus of the new Tyneside Scottish Pipe Band and Drums, under Pipe Major John McFadd and his brother Drum Major Joseph McFadd.

On 25 April 1940 the Tyneside Scottish landed in France along with 10th and 11th Battalions DLI as part of 70th Brigade, 23rd Division. This Division consisted of only two Brigades with no artillery. The role initially assigned to the TS was to assist with airfield construction and complete their training, however, when the Blitzkreig was unleashed less than a month later the Division's role was changed and its men were plunged in at the deep end protecting the BEF's lines of communication. On 17 May, 70th Brigade was ordered forward to take up a defensive position on the Canal du Nord and were sent an additional 11 Light Machine Guns and nine Boys Anti-Tank Rifles to assist them in their task.

The Canal du Nord position proved to be untenable and 70th Brigade was withdrawn eastwards. At Ficheux on 20 May, after some five hours of desperate fighting against the advancing enemy, the Tyneside Scottish were overwhelmed by German forces, which included the 7th Panzer Division under Rommel. 135 TS were killed and the majority of the survivors were taken prisoner. 70th Brigade suffered some of the highest losses of the entire BEF. Only 140 men of the Tyneside Scottish battalion returned to the UK from France in 1940.

The Tyneside Scottish reformed in Devon, receiving drafts of officers and men from the Black Watch. They trained and served as part of the home defence forces during the invasion scares of summer 1940. In October 1940, the 70th Brigade, including the Tyneside Scottish, joined Alabaster Force in Iceland on garrison duties, where it remained until it returned to the UK, landing at Gourock on Christmas morning 1941 and the soldiers were warmly welcomed into the homes of the people of Llanelly to celebrate the day. After three months, the battalion moved to Crickhowell to train as mountain troops on Snowdon. The Brigade found a more permanent 'home' when it became part of 49th (West Riding) Infantry Division on 18 May 1942 and spent their summer camp at Kington, Herefordshire. In September all units in 49 Division took part in Exercise Spartan. It was tough training and the men were getting fed up; although they had been well trained they were not being deployed.

The change came in July 1943 when the TS were despatched to Scotland to train as an assault division. After three years as CO, Lieutenant Colonel Oxley had left to take command of a battalion of the DLI. Lieutenant Colonel 'Jim' Cassels took over and saw the battalion brought up to the highest level of training, but he was rapidly promoted after six months and the TS faced its new challenges with Lieutenant Colonel RWM de Winton of the Gordon Highlanders in command.

After months of hard training the TS moved with their Division to Norfolk with Divisional HQ in Norwich. They had practised manoeuvres across the battle area with the tanks and AFVs of the 7th Armoured Brigade in Thetford. The Tyneside Scottish and the rest of 70 Brigade proceeded to Normandy, where 49 Division was part of the second wave of the invasion force. The majority of the battalion sailed from Newhaven and landed on 12 June 1944 while the battalion's motor transport and support weapons, embarked at West India Docks, London, did not reach Normandy until 16 June. 'R' Company, an additional company, which was formed to provide immediate reinforcements for the Battalion, went to France independently and its personnel were used to replace losses in various units of the 51st (Highland) Division.

The Tyneside Scottish made an abortive attack at Tessel Bretteville on 26 June and on 28 June at Brettevillette, also on the Tilly-sur-Seulles Sector of the British Normandy front. The battalion was involved in a further attack. Although it was successful, sadly the men were unable to hold the land they had taken due to lack of artillery support.

The Battalion earned another 'Battle Honour' at Rauray on 1 July 1944. Almost 30 years previously, on 1 July 1916, the first day of the Battle of the Somme, the Tyneside Scottish had been in the first wave and kept going in waves with all four battalions going 'over the top'. They had suffered horrific losses. The day of 1 July 1944 would be a hard fought one in Normandy too. The lads of the Tyneside Scottish faced the 12th and 26th SS Panzer Divisions as they attempted to break through to the coast. The Tyneside Scottish engaged the enemy with their pipers playing them in. They knocked out approximately 30 tanks and held the feature in the landscape known as 'point 110', but in doing so they suffered terrible losses, repulsing attack after attack. Captain A P Whitehead of the TS wrote:

'As each successive attack broke down the Battalion line, the enemy subjected the whole area, especially the 110 ring contour to murderous artillery and mortar fire, softening up for the next attempt.'

Sleeve insignia worn by the Tyneside Scottish while in 70th Brigade, 49th Division, Normandy 1944.

At the end of the bitterly fought battle the TS had clung on, just over 200 men were left standing, there were over 100 dead and the rest wounded, missing or captured and only one of its six Anti-Tank guns remained fit for use.

Major General Barker sent the following message on the evening of 1 July:

'My congratulations on the magnificent stand made by you today. You have today made a great name for yourselves, not only in the Division, but in the army as a whole. I deplore the casualties you have sustained but am gratified to know that the brilliant band who remained at point 110 were successfully relieved.'

In recognition of their gallantry Rauray was granted as a Battle Honour for the Tyneside Scottish.

Reinforcements from the South Wales Borderers, Herefords, Essex and Gloucesters brought the TS back up to strength and the battalion was sent forward again to Juvigny on the Tilly-sur-Seulles Sector and later at Caen. When the Germans made a withdrawal mid-August, the Tyneside Scottish moved forward with the general advance, reaching Mezidon but the days of 70th Brigade were numbered. After the losses suffered by so many infantry battalions in the 21st Army there needed to be a rationalisation process and 70th Brigade was one of those that was disbanded. Between 23 and 24 August 1944 the men were drawn off to reinforce other units, mostly in 51st (Highland) Division and 50th (Northumbrian) Division. The 1st Battalion, Tyneside Scottish went into suspended animation. The Tyneside Scottish Association carried on, there were Regimental reunions and dinners, but the battalion was not raised again until 1946 and this time it was to be as a Territorial Army artillery unit. Today its descendant unit is still going strong as 204 Battery, 101st (Northumbrian) Regiment, Royal Artillery and they are still very proud to be 'Geordie Jocks.'

The 50th (Northumbrian) Division

The two red letter 'T's on a black background, the divisional insignia that recognised the great rivers, The Tyne and the Tees (the two Ts also form an H for Humber) that run through their main recruitment areas for 50th Division – Northumberland, Durham and Yorkshire. This sign, painted on vehicles and worn as cloth insignia on the upper arms of the soldiers that served within the Division became the emblem of one of the most famous units of the Second World War, with a hard fighting war record second to none.

The 50 Division was a motorised division made up of both infantry and corps from the Territorial Army with three infantry brigades (each Brigade would usually contain three battalions of soldiers and an anti-tank company), the 151st Infantry Brigade was 6th, 8th, 9th

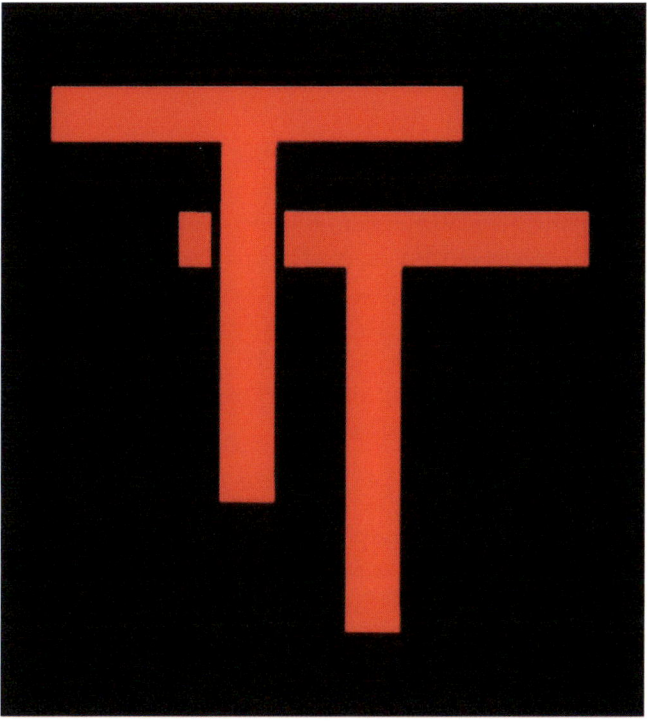

The famous 'TT' formation sign of the 50th (Northumbrian) Division

Geordie lads from the corps units of the 50th Division paused for the camera in the Cotswold country of Oxfordshire while they were completing their training for overseas service, 1939

Battalions, Durham Light Infantry but it was the Divisional Troops that drew its men from Newcastle and Northumberland, specifically the Divisional Artillery included 72nd and 74th (Northumbrian) Field Regiments, Royal Artillery; Divisional Engineers that included 232nd (Northumbrian) and 505th (Field Company) and 235th (Northumbrian) Field Park Company, Royal Engineers and the 4th Battalion, Royal Northumberland Fusiliers. There were also plenty of Geordie and Tyneside lads in the other Divisional units of Royal Army Medical Corps, Royal Signals and Royal Army Service Corps. Many lads who served in the Division had worked as miners or in the shipyards before the outbreak of war.

Some of the battalions of 50 Division had only been in existence since the expansion of the Territorial Army in 1938, others for just a matter of months when they were mobilized on the day Germany invaded Poland, 1 September 1939. In October, the division was concentrated in the Cotswold country of Oxfordshire to complete training for overseas service. The problem was that training was hampered by a lack of uniforms and equipment and when they finally deployed to join the British Expeditionary Force in France on 19 January 1940, a number of large deliveries of the long-awaited equipment were made to their former billets, which led to yet more problems.

The Division was soon sent for intensive training in the Amiens area and was deployed in reserve near Loos in late March. The men spent most of their time constructing anti-tank obstacles, pill boxes and defences; an ideal task for North country men who knew how to work with pick and shovel and wasted no time stripping to the waist and setting to. They completed the job faster than any other Division, including those that had the benefit of mechanical excavators.

On 9 May Hitler unleashed the Blitzkrieg and advanced at a frightening speed into France. 50 Division was sent to take a defensive position on the River Dendre behind Brussels, but the advance of the blitzkrieg was such that the British army was left reeling and was rapidly making a fighting retreat to the coast. 50 Division initially received orders to withdraw too and the divisional engineers prepared all their bridges across the Dendre and Escaut line for demolition.

As the fraught days passed, it soon appeared the BEF might be cut off near Arras and 50 Division were sent there to make a counter attack. On 21 May one Brigade and divisional troops were ordered to attack, supported by tanks, in what became known as the Battle of Arras. The lads of the Durham Light Infantry and Northumberland Fusiliers fought hard as part of what is recognised as the first British vs German tank battle of the Second World War. The attack, against tanks under the command of Rommel, was successful, an advance of some 10 miles through enemy territory had been achieved, heavy casualties had been inflicted on the enemy and over 400 prisoners had been taken. More than twenty enemy tanks had also been destroyed, two of which were accounted for by Fusilier Christopher Wilson who managed to take them out with his anti-tank gun, a feat of courage and skill for which he was awarded the Military Medal.

The advance, however, could not be sustained, the Germans launched heavy attacks by dive bombers and the enemy tanks opened up on the division's armoured support. It was clear the enemy was much superior in strength and a further attack was cancelled. The BEF was now cut off from the bulk of the French armies, and had no other option than to begin its retreat towards Dunkirk. 50 Division was withdrawn from Arras to near Loos and Ypres where it provided a rearguard for the eastern flank of the BEF, suffering heavy casualties as it did so. On 28 May 1940, 50 Division received orders to withdraw and began their fighting retreat to La Panne to be evacuated. But at the

Members of 505 Field Engineer Company (Newcastle) manhandling a small box girder bridge over a river crossing during an exercise in 1941

eleventh hour they were ordered to draw back to occupy a sector for the Franco-Belgian frontier. The men of 50 Division had been fighting almost continuously since 21 May and they faced a ferocious attack. Other areas were penetrated in the line but as the history of 50 Division put it: *'the grim fighting qualities of these North country troops restored the situation.'* Over the night of 31 May to 1 June what remained of 50 Division withdrew across the French frontier to a position south of Bray Dunes and evacuated. The last of the divisional troops left on the night of 2 June. 50 Division was the last division to leave from Dunkirk.

On its return to the UK 50 Division was directed to a large camp near Knutsford, Cheshire to rebuild itself and was then moved to Dorset to prepare and man the anti-invasion defences from Lyme Regis to Christchurch. In September 1941 the seniors officers of the Division were informed they had been

Senior NCOs from 505 Field Engineer Company, back from Dunkirk and ready for foreign service. The issue of khaki drill and pith helmets certainly drew many a joke as demonstrated by 'six shooter' Sgt Billy Chape of Heaton.

earmarked as the first Territorial Division to be deployed to North Africa when the time came. On 12 December 1940, 50 Division moved to the north coast of Somerset where they remained in an anti-invasion role.

In the spring of 1941 the men were warned of deployment abroad and speculation went wild when they were issued with uniform for tropical climates. On 21 April 1941 Advanced Divisional Headquarters and 150 Brigade Group set off for their embarkation port of Liverpool. The remainder of the division, containing many of the Geordie troops, sailed from Glasgow a month later. This group sailed in Convoy WS. 8 aboard a former liner, the SS Orduna. A few days into the voyage there was a problem with the ship's gearing that caused a collision with another ship in the convoy. The noise of the strike caused many men on board to fear they had been torpedoed. The damage caused Orduna to slow down and the rest of the convoy decided to sail on while repairs were made. This left crew and troops on board feeling very vulnerable without an escort but they eventually continued their journey, fascinated by the shoals of dolphins they saw on their way to Freetown (Sierra Leone) with a brief stop in Durban (South Africa). It was only later they found out that while they had been out on the ocean alone the Bismark was only 32 sailing hours to their North.

Orduna finally reached Port Tewfick, Egypt under fire. The men had not been told to change into tropical kit so they disembarked wearing battledress, carrying their greatcoats, kit bags, equipment, gas masks, helmets and rifles into a temperature of 110 degrees. The men recalled the sweat dripped off them like raindrops as they marched down the gangplank. They spent two weeks in Ismalia, then on 26 July 1941 they set sail for Cyprus where they were dispersed over a large area, constructing defences, especially around the airport and city of Nicosia. Reunited in July, the division continued its work until 3 November when they left for Palestine and proceeded to Northern Iraq where they spent the winter. At Christmas in Kirkuk the concert party put on a pantomime in a wet marquee by the light of oil lamps. Most people would imagine the country to be one of sweltering hot, sandy desert but it was so cold even eggs froze in their shells and the ground froze so hard it made the burying of mines on the border with Turkey very difficult.

In January 1942, 50 Division was ordered to Syria to relieve the 6th Australian Division in the Baalbek area for three weeks, after which they embarked on a 10-day, 2000 mile journey by truck and train, passing through Tuz, Tel Aviv, Ismalia, and Cairo. They crossed the Nile and passed the pyramids and continued through the desert to the Gazala line west of Torbuk. As they progressed further into the desert, they saw grim reminders that they were in a war zone. Graves of friend and foe punctuated the route, each cemetery seeming to become larger as they got closer to the front, they saw burnt out tanks and various forms of abandoned transport. Every night the sky was lit as Torbuk was attacked and the roar of the guns could be heard.

The men of the 50 Division distinguished themselves at the Battle of Gazala in May 1942 and, after the surrender of Tobruk, on 21 June 1942, a new defensive line was made south of the port of Mersa Matruh. Matruh was a small camp on the Egyptian coast, well known to 1 Battalion, Royal Northumberland Fusiliers

Pte Adam Wakenshaw, 9th Battalion, Durham Light Infantry. The first man from Newcastle to receive the Victoria Cross during the Second World War.

who were there shortly before the outbreak of war in 1939. When 50 Division arrived in the area it was a war zone and they dug in as best they could on an escarpment. Once again, already weary from weeks of fighting, the men of the Division were called upon to fight heavy defensive battle against an enemy of superior numbers and resources.

On 27 June 1942 the Germans attempted to pass the escarpment and the attack was pressed heavily against the men of 9th Battalion, Durham Light Infantry and 50 Division. The situation was critical and it is such times that soldiers truly show their mettle. Many acts of heroism were not recorded, but one DLI soldier went above and beyond that day. The Newcastle-born former coal miner Private Adam Wakenshaw (28), 9th Battalion, Durham Light Infantry was a member of the crew of a 2-pounder anti-tank gun when an enemy vehicle towing a light gun came within short range and his gun opened fire. Private Wakenshaw succeeded in immobilising the enemy vehicle but another mobile gun came into action and killed or seriously wounded everyone in Wakenshaw's gun crew. His citation picks up the story: *'Under intense fire, Private Wakenshaw crawled back to his gun. Although his left arm was blown off, he loaded the gun with one arm and fired five more rounds, setting the tractor on fire and damaging the light gun. A direct hit on the ammunition finally killed him and destroyed the gun. This act of conspicuous gallantry prevented the enemy from using their light gun on the infantry Company which was only 200 yards away. It was through the self sacrifice and courageous devotion to duty of this infantry anti-tank gunner that the Company was enabled to withdraw in safety.'*

Private Adam Wakenshaw was posthumously awarded the Victoria Cross, our nation's highest gallantry medal, for actions in the presence of the enemy. He was the first of a total of four VC awards to 50 Division and was the first Newcastle man to be awarded the VC in the Second World War. He is buried in the El Alamein War Cemetery.

By the end of the action at Mersa Matruh the 50 Division had suffered over 9,000 casualties since the start of the fighting at Gazala, its equipment was becoming war worn or had been destroyed by action but by mid-July they had received reinforcements and they fought on, notably at the Second Battle of El Alamein where 151 Brigade took their turn in the front line again.

In October 1942 another notable local unit, the 102nd (Northumberland Hussars) Anti-Tank Regiment joined 50 Division in October 1942. 50 Division fought on through the later battles in North Africa then on to Sicily in July 1942 and returned to Britain, sailing up the Mersey Estuary on the misty, rainy morning of 2 November 1943. After all they had gone through there was no heroes' welcome as there was a blackout on the

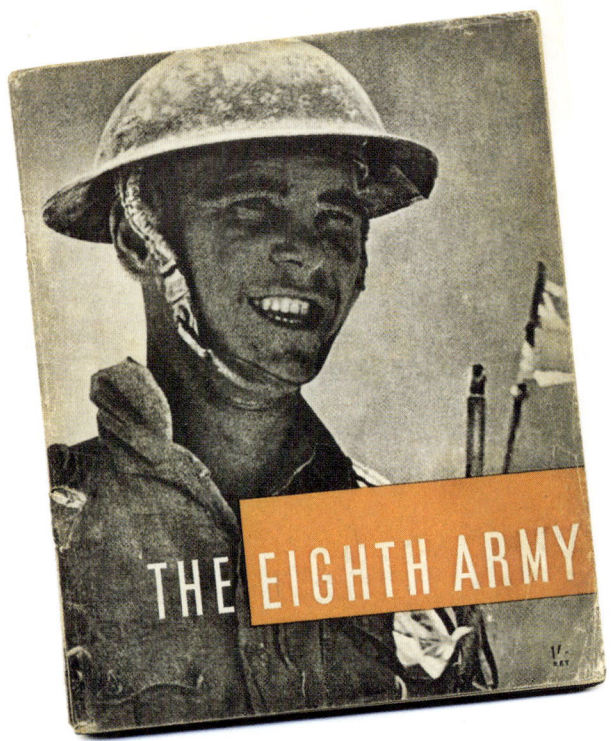

reporting of the movement of the Division and the men marched down the gang planks to a city ignorant of their return.

Over the next 36 hours, the units of 50 Division made their way to the Norfolk and Suffolk borders with Divisional Headquarters established at Chadacre Park, near Bury St Edmunds. After just two weeks' leave they began training for 'something big.' Now part of XXX Corps, assault brigades were sent for specialist training at the No1 Combined Training Centre on the remote shores of Loch Fyne, Inveraray, Scotland over the winter. In April, 50 Division moved to the south coast where they began a series of large-scale exercises practising beach landings at Studland Bay, Dorset.

50 Division had been reinforced by the 56th Infantry Brigade, the 8th Armoured Brigade, 47th Royal Marine

Commandos, two further artillery regiments and four batteries and supporting arms including two Beach Groups. The Divisional Commander, Major General Douglas Graham, sent a special D-Day message to all ranks of 50 Division:

'The time is at hand to strike – to break the Western Wall and into the Continent of Europe. To you, officers and men of the 50th (Northumbrian) Division, has been given the great honour of being in the vanguard of the mighty blow for freedom ... Much has been asked of you in the past and great have been your achievements but this will be the greatest adventure of all.'

Their destination was the Normandy beaches in the first wave of the assault on Gold Beach (the area between the fortified villages of Le Hammel and La Rivière), D-Day, 6 June 1944. Their success was one of the keys to the overall success of Operation Overlord, for they were to widen and deepen the bridgehead and secure Arromanches to enable the deployment of the Mulberry harbour and then fight on to Caen. After being the last Division out of Dunkirk, they would return among the first to land on D-Day. The memories of the landings remained vivid in the minds of all who were there, every man could feel the tightness of fear in his belly but, having come through Dunkirk, North Africa and Sicily, many old soldiers did feel confident the D-Day landings would be successful. A number of veterans said that after the time they had spent on the landing craft being sick and watching their friends throw up too, their boots becoming slippery because of the vomit, they were just glad to be off and out of the landing craft.

The task was not easy, danger was ever present and every man had to do his bit; there were many heroes on that day but it is worthy of note that CSM Stan Hollis, 6th Battalion, Green Howards, serving in 50 Division was the only man to be decorated with a Victoria Cross for his gallantry on D-Day. The advance to Caen,

Top: Beach Group troops file past the line of 50th Division lorries on Gold Beach, 7 June 1944. Above: The road inland from Gold Beach, Normandy has been renamed 50th (Northumbrian) Division Way

A privately produced souvenir postcard to the mark the significant battles fought by 50th (Northumbrian) Division, 1942-1945

however, failed in its first push and warfare descended into what became known as 'the battle of the hedgerows' where every ditch, hedge, wood and village between the beaches and Caen was hard fought for and costly in lives.

50 Division advanced to the Falaise Pocket and reached a stalemate that was only broken by hard fighting. Onward they marched again to the Low Countries and Operation Market Garden where, as British troops hung on at Arnhem, XXX Corps, including 50 Division, hastened to relieve them. On 1 October 1944 the Germans blocked the relief column on the Nijmegen Salient. 50 Division's 124 Field Regiment fired continuously from 0400hrs to 2300 hr, firing a total of 12,500 rounds during the action. Opposition was stiff but objectives had been captured by 6 October. 50 Division was then moved to another sector of the bridgehead on the Neder Rijn and the Waal, known as 'The Island.' Their time from then on was spent on static warfare and the men got to know this area of low-lying fields and orchards of apples and pears criss-crossed with dykes where they kept an eye over the bridge at Nijmegen. Here, at night, the men would sometimes see what some might have thought were shooting stars, except they were moving upwards. They were in fact V2 rockets being fired against England.

Problems reinforcing 21st Army Group were solved by it being reduced by one Division and 50 Division was selected to go; they were withdrawn to Belgium on 29 November 1944 the division's fighting career ended. Overall they had lost 488 officers and there were 6,932 casualties among the other ranks since the Normandy landings. They had also taken more than 17,202 enemy prisoners.

A skeleton Division returned to Yorkshire to train men of other arms as infantrymen. Many of those who had served three and half years or more were given the option of demobilization or garrison duties, others were given generous periods of leave and those who remained were deployed to new units. There were very few men left in 50 Division who could say they answered the call in 1939 and were still serving with the division and fewer still who had come through without a scratch.

Royal Navy

Growing up on Tyneside watching so many great ships launched and being given time off school to watch the latest proud vessel sail up the Tyne, it is hardly surprising that thousands of local lads felt inspired to join the Royal Navy and see more of the world than shipyards or mines.

A number of men from Tyneside were recognised for their gallantry during the evacuations of British and French troops from the French coast in 1940, among them are Petty Officer William Leece (26), whose mother lived on Rochester Street, Walker, who was awarded the Distinguished Service Medal for his bravery while serving aboard HMS *Ventia* on 23 May 1940. HMS *Ventia* steamed over the Channel with sister Destroyers *Venomous* and *Wild Swan* to rescue soldiers of the Guards who had become surrounded during the Battle of Boulogne. *Ventia* attracted shell fire from heavy guns of the coastal battery causing her briefly to go out of control and beach. With casualties on the bridge and having sustained several hits from the shells, the crew of *Ventia* did not give up and although she did not manage to rescue any troops she had drawn the fire so that others could. *Ventia* quickly refloated and reversed out of the harbour at full speed, returning to Britain where she was repaired and was deployed to active service again.

Another Tyneside hero of the Dunkirk evacuation was Royal Navy Gunner T W Watson (21) of High Felling, whose Liverpool steamer was ordered to proceed to Dunkirk in May 1940. As she passed other vessels, she was warned not to continue but her Captain decided to press on regardless. Gunner Watson was at his post on the bridge when an enemy plane dropped a bomb 50ft away, hitting a ship that began to sink. The plane circled and then made for Watson's ship on two more occasions but each time he was driven off by Watson's gunfire. The ship carried on and the crew did not rest for 48 hours but they did what they came to do. The Captain, chief engineer and chief officer were all awarded Distinguished Service Crosses and our Felling hero was presented with a Distinguished Service Medal for bravery in the action.

HMS King George V moored outside the Vickers Armstrong Naval Yard, in Walker where she was launched in 1939

During the course of the war, Geordie and Tyneside lads were to be found among the crews of many of the Royal Navy vessels involved in some of the most significant actions of the war. They were some of the crew lost at the infamous sinking of HMS *Hood* in 1941 and were among the crew of the HMS *King George V*, built at the Vickers-Armstrong shipyard on the Tyne, one of the vessels that avenged the *Hood* by hunting and sinking the *Bismark* in May 1941. Another notable ship built on the Tyne was HMS *Victorious*, the 23,000-ton aircraft carrier built at the Walker Naval Yard of Vickers Armstrong. She also took her part in the *Bismark* kill, aircraft launched from her decks armed with torpedoes scored at least one hit on the vessel.

One of the most remarkable stories relates not to a member of the Royal Navy but sixteen-year-old Thomas William 'Tommy' Brown of North Shields, who was a Junior Canteen Assistant in the NAAFI aboard the Royal Navy Destroyer HMS *Petard*. On 30 October 1942 *Petard* was in water just of Port Said, Egypt when Royal Navy vessels had attacked and damaged the German submarine U-559 so that it surfaced. Firing her 4-inch guns, the *Petard* delivered the coup de grace and the U-boat crew abandoned ship. Aware the codebooks for U-boat Enigma would still be on board, a boarding party crossed in a boat to see if they could retrieve them. However the crew of U-559 had opened its seacocks and water was pouring in.

Jedburgh Grammar School educated Royal Navy Lieutenant Tony Fasson and Able Seaman Colin Grazier thought they would at least try to get the code books, so they stripped off, dived into the sea and swam to fetch them with Tommy Brown following close behind.

Working in pitch darkness, Fasson and Grazier located the code books and passed them to Tommy, who carried them up the iron ladder of the U-Boat's conning tower to the boat. As he did so he saw the water was pouring in at a dangerous rate and warned Fasson and Grazier to get out, but she sank suddenly with both men on board, dragging Tommy down too. He managed to fight his way back to the surface but his two shipmates were not so lucky.

The code books provided they key that enabled the code breakers at Bletchley Park to break U-Boat Enigma codes. Both Fasson and Grazier were awarded George Crosses and Tommy Brown was awarded the George Medal for his bravery and he remains one of the youngest recipients of the award. Tragically Tommy died from injuries he sustained while on leave as he attempted to rescue his sister Maureen (4) from a fire at their family home in Lily Gardens, Ridges Estate, North Shields on 13 February 1945. He was buried with full naval honours at Preston Cemetery.

Royal Air Force

There were very few units that didn't have at least one lad they all knew as 'Geordie' and the RAF was no exception.

Among Newcastle and Tyneside's roll of RAF heroes are recipients of the Distinguished Flying Cross (DFC) and Distinguished Flying Medal (DFM), including one of the first to be decorated, Durham-born Newcastle Breweries trainee Flying Officer Anthony 'Bunny' Forster, serving with 607 Squadron. At 26 he was a veteran of the Battle of France and was still serving during The Battle of Britain. He was awarded the Distinguished Flying Cross in July 1940, credited with shooting down six enemy aircraft, four of them over France. He survived the war and retired a Wing Commander in 1962.

Wing Commander Richard Angus McMurtrie DFC of Monkseaton earned a Distinguished Service Order while serving with 269 Squadron for leading three bombing missions over five days, flying over 60 miles of enemy occupied territory in Norway in 1940.

'Dambuster' Pilot Officer Ivan Whittaker, was born in Walkerville and educated at Wallsend Grammar School. He gained his DFC while a member of 617 Squadron as the flight engineer on the third Lancaster to attack the Möhne Dam. He was awarded a Bar for his DFC in 1944 for the careful handling of his aircraft's engine that enable a safe landing after it had been damaged by shell fire during an attack on the Antheor viaduct in Southern France. He is believed to be the only flight engineer to have received the DFC and Bar.

Wing Commander Lionel Cohen was still flying on active service missions as Observer or Air Gunner aged 68. Some nicknamed him 'Evergreen' in his Squadron but it was 'Sos', short for Sausage, to those who knew

RAF 83 Maintenance Unit dance band from RAF Woolsington, Newcastle 1941

him best. He was born at Tankerville House, Tankerville Terrace in Newcastle in 1875, son of the distinguished Anglo-Jewish family of ship owner Andrew Cohen. Sos always sought adventure so he enlisted in the Royal Marine Light Infantry and saw his first active service in the Matabeleland Campaign of 1893. He operated behind enemy lines during the South African War and earned the rank of Captain and both

Taking Off, a popular illustrated booklet among young lads with dreams of becoming a fighter pilot during the war

the Military Cross and the Distinguished Service Order in the South African Horse during the First World War. During the Great War he had a secondment to the Royal Naval Air Service. Between the wars he worked as stockbroker in London but when the rumbles of war began in 1930s Sos was instrumental in the creation of the Royal Air Force Volunteer Reserve and it is a testimony to his remarkable energy, eyesight, excellent marksmanship and exceptional physical fitness that enabled him to pass the gruelling aircrew test. Sos flew over seventy operational flights over Iceland, North Africa and North Western Europe and accrued over 500 hours flying in convoy escort aircraft over the Atlantic.

In February 1944 it was announced he had been awarded the Distinguished Flying Cross *'for gallantry and devotion to duty in air operations.'* He received it with his typical modesty, saying that he accepted it 'for those incredible youngsters of Coastal Command with whom I fly. I have been sufficiently honoured simply by being allowed to keep such company … they are the salt of the earth.' Sos survived the war, indeed some called him 'the man with a hundred lives,' and passed away in August 1960 aged 86.

Prisoners of War

War can lead to some remarkable coincidences. Men in far-flung corners of the world in desert and jungle would hear the unmistakable Geordie accent and discover a pal from the Toon. Duncan McPherson and Ken Stokes grew up in Heaton. They both attended the Royal Grammar School and then found employment in the Town Clerk's department of Newcastle Corporation. When the call came to do their bit, Duncan joined the Royal Engineers and Ken joined the Tyneside Scottish. Both were taken prisoner during the fighting in France in May 1940 and they ended up in prisoner of war camps in Poland but they were many miles apart. McPherson had a good knowledge of German and French, he also had some knowledge of Italian and Spanish so he was appointed camp interpreter. His workload was heavy and was another interpreter was sought in other prison camps. A suitable

Still able to raise a smile, some of the British Prisoners of War incarcerated at Stalag VIII B, at Lamsdorf, Silesia

man was found; imagine McPherson's surprise when in walked his old pal Ken Stokes.

As the war progressed POW camps got larger and larger; there were even a number of camps for German and Italian prisoners in Northumberland. Many youngsters growing up in the countryside near these camps have happy memories of the prisoners they encountered working in the fields. As the numbers of British POWs in Germany also grew, one camp seemed to have far more prisoners from the North East than any other, indeed by 1943 Stalag VIIIB near Lamsdorf, Silesia had so many they began a Northumberland and Durham POW Association in the camp! Their aims were to provide newly arrived prisoners with clothing, books and comforts. News of the association had come home in a letters from Wireless Operator Serjeant R J Fletcher to his wife on Strathmore Road, Gosforth. He explained he was one of the founders of the association and was proud to say they had already achieved a membership of 300 and were enrolling more. Once the Northumberland and Durham War Needs Fund heard

Red Cross and St John Prisoners of War Department leaflet on food parcels, January 1941

of the POW Association, they quickly pledged their support in a letter signed by the Lord Mayor of Newcastle.

Other lads were not so fortunate and were in POW camps where they suffered deliberately poor treatment for their wounds or infections and were brutalised by

Notification sent to the family of Gunner Aaron Wilson at Benwell that her son was presumed a prisoner of war, July 1942

their guards. When the Allies grew near to liberating some of the camps between January and April 1945, the prisoners, even those who were sick or injured, were forced to march west across Poland, Czechoslovakia and Germany in bitter winter conditions. Among them were lads from Newcastle who had been in the British POW section of the notorious Auschwitz concentration camp. Around 80,000 prisoners were forced to march in this way and thousands of them died en-route.

After Liberation came medics and welfare officers. Among those who arrived at Sandbostel Concentration Camp in north-western Germany was Wallsend-born Red Cross Welfare Officer Miss Paddy Arthur (24). She recalled the camp had 12,000 civilian prisoners from a variety of countries in occupied Europe: *'The dead lay side-by-side with the living, who were themselves virtual skeletons.'* The place came to be known as 'Little Belsen.'

Far Eastern Prisoners of War

Many believed that 9th Battalion, Royal Northumberland Fusiliers, was a jinxed battalion. The original 9th Battalion had been the second Kitchener Battalion raised in Newcastle and had suffered heavy casualties like many active service battalions, but in the Second World War the story was that the original 9th Battalion in the Great War had been wiped out. The battalion's first experience of the Second World War was in France in 1940 those who believed in the curse and felt that it was still active. Those lucky enough to evacuate left under gunfire. The battalion was rebuilt and embarked for the Middle East but was diverted to defend Singapore. After leaving their last action under fire many they knew this one would be worse because they were entering under gunfire this time. The 9 RNF landed at Singapore on 5 February 1942 and joined the bitter fighting to defend the island until the surrender just nine days later on 14 February. Men of the battalion, along with thousands of others also captured at the fall of Singapore, were held by the Japanese until the allies' final victory in the Far East in September 1945. Many of these men suffered mental and physical injuries for the rest of their lives from the maltreatment they received while prisoners of war.

Women in Uniformed Services

The Royal Navy, Auxiliary Territorial Service and Royal Air Force had women's branches and, just like the men of the North, women of Newcastle, Northumberland and Tyneside made a significant contribution to all three.

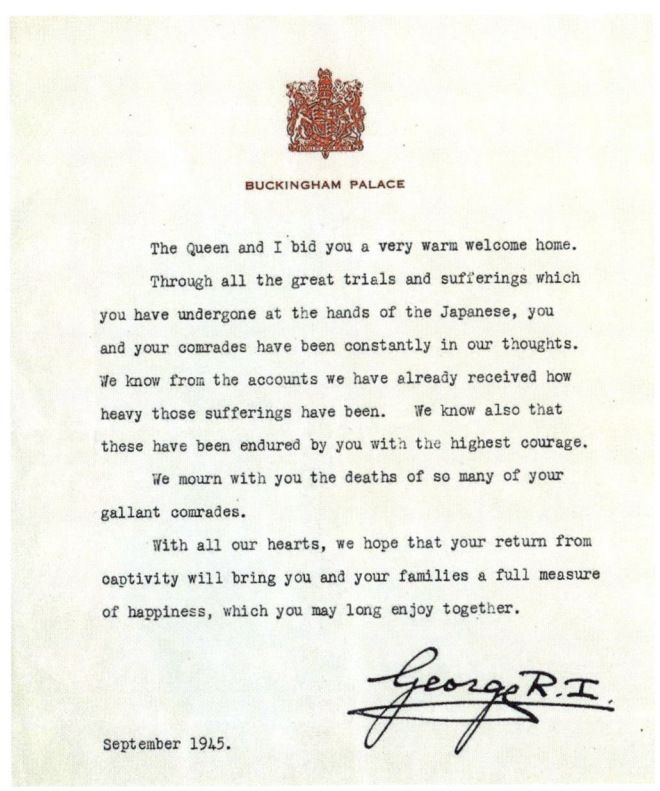 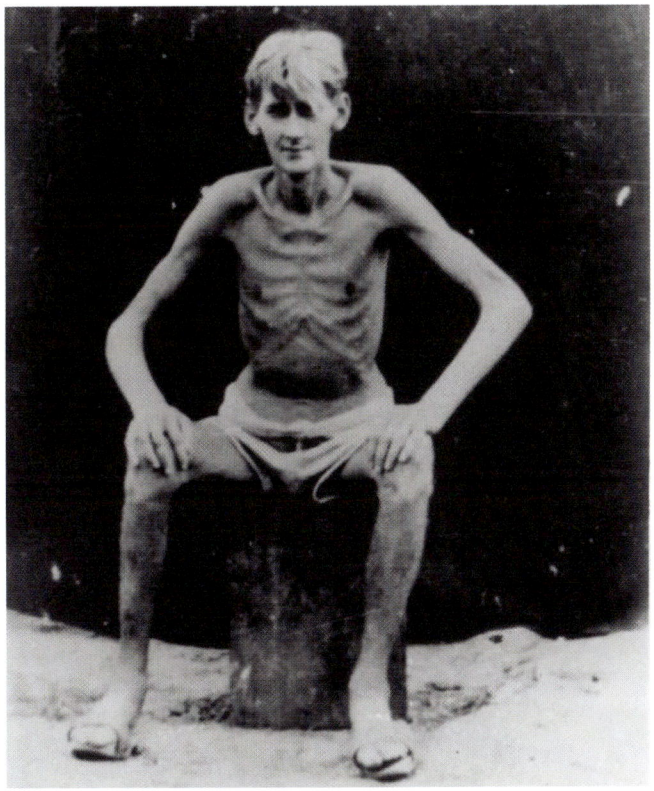

Left: Welcome home letter with printed signature of King George VI sent from Buckingham Palace to those who returned from years of Japanese captivity. Right: One of thousands of malnourished British prisoners of war being forced to labour while in Japanese hands

As a city by one of the most important rivers of Britain, Newcastle had a Royal Navy presence before and during the Second World War and from 1939 they had members of the Women's Royal Naval Service to support them. Wrens also provided staff at Royal Navy bases along the coast, such as the depot ship HMS *Titania*, 6th Submarine Flotilla, Blyth, at Tynemouth, North Shields and at the RN 'Y' Service Stations in the county for the interception of enemy military radio transmissions.

In January 1941, just before conscription was introduced for women, Lady Charlotte Rous, Officer in Charge of recruiting for the Women's Auxiliary Air Force (WAAF) in the Northern Area proudly announced that the number of volunteers for service in the WAAF was higher in the Newcastle and Tyneside area than in any other region in the UK. Members of the WAAF worked in a host of administrative roles, drove ambulances and helped rearm and keep aircraft running on airfields but are best known for their work as plotters in the operations rooms at air fields, including 'RAF Newcastle', the headquarters of No 13 Group Royal Air Force Fighter Command at Kenton Bar from 1940-1944. Newcastle and Tyneside were targets for numerous bombing raids and one of the best ways to foil enemy aircraft was by keeping them up high and even away by using barrage balloons. The majority

The Duchess of Kent, Commandant of the Women's Royal Naval Service (far right) inspecting Wrens at North Shields during her visit to three centres in the North East, October 1940 Left: Women's Auxiliary Air Force Barrage Balloon operators, Park View, Heaton, 1941

of barrage balloon sites in Newcastle and Tyneside were crewed by members of the WAAF.

A much smaller unit was the Air Transport Auxiliary, which provided ferry pilots to transport newly built aircraft from factories to operational airfields, although female pilots were only permitted to deliver the aircraft to UK bases. There was always a waiting list, but one of those accepted was Rhoda Hepple of Matthew Bank, daughter of the Newcastle Flying Club chairman, Squadron Leader Philip Forsyth Heppell. Rhoda was first engaged by the ATA in December 1941. After just eight hours' instruction she began flying the first of 17 different types of aircraft to Air Ministry centres.

The first major recruitment event for women's services in Newcastle was staged in February 1941, when a contingent of 200 ATS marched through Newcastle to Brunswick Place, headed by the band of the Royal Northumberland Fusiliers. The march was to herald the opening of an ATS recruiting exhibition by the Duchess of Northumberland at Fenwicks. Their aim was for Newcastle and Northumberland to raise some of the 20,000 recruits (aged between seventeen and a half and forty-three, ex-service women could join up to age forty-nine) who were wanted to release soldiers from non-combatant duties. The exhibition featured many aspects of service life in the ATS and showed off a specimen of uniform, which, the newspapers noted, included *'first-quality shoes such as few girls buy in private life.'*

Later in the month Bainbridge's hosted a major recruiting event for the Motor Transport Corps. The MTC was a volunteer women's organisation started in London, which spread through the provinces providing units of drivers to the War Office, Admiralty, Air Ministry or any other war organisation that needed them. Every volunteer underwent an intensive training course in drill, convoy driving, car maintenance, map reading and first aid. The aim of the recruiting event at Bainbridge's was to establish a strong divisional unit for the North Eastern Counties. Recruiting was brisk and some women offered to use their own cars, for which they were allowed 3d a mile after buying their petrol and oil.

March 1941 saw conscription for women for the first time in British history. The Act required compulsory Registration for Employment for unmarried women aged eighteen to forty-five from March 1941. Subsequently married women were included and the age limit was increased to fifty; the only exceptions being pregnant women and mothers with children under fourteen living with them. Thousands of women had joined either civilian or military uniformed services before conscription was introduced but, in the spirit of one volunteer is worth ten pressed men (or women), the various services were keen to attract the pick of the women before conscription enforced service and

Newcastle NAAFI staff 1941

Members of the Auxiliary Territorial Service serving in Anti-Aircraft Command at Birtley, October 1941. Left: Eileen Bishop 'The Ideal NAAFI Girl' visited Newcastle as part of a recruitment drive for NAAFI staff in April 1942

recruitment events were staged in large towns and cities around the country.

In April 1942 the women's services recruitment drive in Newcastle was for the Navy, Army and Air Force Institutes (NAAFI). An official welcome from Lord Mayor George Dixon was extended to Miss Eileen Bishop, who had been selected from 30,000 as the 'Ideal NAAFI Girl' to tour the country as the public face of the organisation during its recruitment campaign. In her speech she spoke of the work of NAAFI and how much the snacks and sandwiches they provided were appreciated by all in the services. During the recruitment drive NAAFI was hoping to recruit 600 girls a week. It was estimated that on average throughout the course of the war the NAAFI served around 3.5 million cups of tea every day. Indeed, when NAAFI workers were presented with awards for their gallantry they were described as the 'Cup of Tea Heroes.'

The Auxiliary Territorial Service had been raised back in September 1938 (originally titled the WATS – Women's Auxiliary Territorial Service), usually designated 40th Company for its affiliation to infantry regiments. A WATS company was affiliated to the Royal Northumberland Fusiliers in Newcastle and a company was also formed at Gateshead, affiliated to 9th Battalion, Durham Light Infantry early in 1939. The WATS service company in Newcastle was rapidly up to capacity and the Companies at Blyth and Alnwick were the first to be recruited to full strength in Northumberland, closely followed by the Berwick Company, affiliated to 7th Battalion, Royal Northumberland Fusiliers. The *St George's Gazette* for June 1939 recorded:

'Our WATS have been of great assistance to us for the past two months; the cooks and dining hall sections have been attended three times a week and have been carrying out the duties of our regular personnel. The clerical and storekeeper sections have been attending for instruction every Thursday evening ... They all show great enthusiasm.'

On the outbreak of war, the women of the Royal Northumberland Fusiliers 40th Company were mobilized and accommodated in Fenham Barracks. There the 19th Training Centre was established where many girls would experience their first three weeks of drill and basic training before progressing to their trades and proficiencies. During a visit in March 1940, ATS Chief Controller Dame Helen Gwynne-Vaughan described women from the North as ideal recruits *'because they can stick at work so well. They are good workers, are possessed of strong characters and can stand up to conditions which are not always too easy in the army.'*

When the Princess Royal came to Fenham Barracks on a tour of inspection in April 1940, she was shown how all the items required by a recruit from stores, from braces to cap badge, were issued by the ATS storekeepers in just 50 seconds. Her Royal Highness also visited separate companies of the ATS, and spoke to Miss Gwen Muter, from Bedlington Colliery, who had worked in a Newcastle jeweller's office before she joined the ATS. Before the Princess Royal left, she visited the ATS recreation room and watched the women doing crafts and playing darts.

The Auxiliary Territorial Service also provided crews and staff for Anti-Aircraft Command gun sites around Newcastle, Northumberland and Tyneside, becoming the biggest presence of any women's military arm in the area and The Duchess of Northumberland's Comforts Fund for the ATS was created to support them.

Allies from Near and Far

Newcastle welcomed service personnel from all over the UK and allies from some far-flung corners of the world.

On a local level, the defences of the Tyne protecting the shipyards, industries, city and towns needed to be able to resist any threat from the air. The stalwarts of the Tyne Electrical Engineers had been operating their searchlights for years, but as more old units were converted to AA roles and more new units were being formed from the later 1930s to join them, more were required. During the Battle of Britain and Blitz of 1941 there were over 50 Heavy and Light Anti-Aircraft gunner and searchlight units from the 7th Anti-Aircraft Division serving on the Tyne defences. The units and

NAAFI Mobile Libraries and Tea Cars in Newcastle 1942

Multi-view postcard of the Newcastle NAAFI Club c1942

their volunteers came from Northumberland and Durham and further afield including Belfast, Lincolnshire and Scotland.

Troops from all over Britain and Europe were sent to Northumberland for training, re-equipping and engaged in all manner of roles on land sea and in the air. In 1942 Newcastle became the first British port to provide a rest centre for Dutch seamen. Polish troops in training on the borders with Scotland would make visits to Newcastle and enjoy hospitality from the members of the Newcastle Friends of Poland Society, who would bring together Polish refugees in Newcastle and servicemen for get togethers in the city. RAF Squadrons and Squadrons from Allied Countries serving in the UK were also based in Northumberland. Looking along the rows of headstones in the Commonwealth War Graves section of Chevington Cemetery reveals fallen aircrew who came from Canada, Australia, New Zealand, Poland, Czechoslovakia, Netherlands and Jamaica serving at RAF Acklington. When America joined the war, the 225th Anti-Aircraft Artillery Searchlight Battalion 'The Skylighters' were also based in Blyth and over 200 square miles of Tyneside in March 1944. The Battalion left Blyth in May 1944 then proceeded to Omaha Beach in June 1944.

FOR U.S. ARMED FORCES IN U.K.

Newcastle upon Tyne

To all branches of the Armed Forces of the United States of America visiting Newcastle I extend a most warm welcome and trust their stay in the City will be a happy and enjoyable one.

Newcastle is an ancient and historic City and has many interesting associations with the past. Its engineering works and shipyards, which at present are producing war equipment to full capacity, are amongst the most modern in the country.

Whilst extending this welcome, I am not unmindful of the many generous gifts received by the City from the people of the United States, for which we are very grateful.

Thomas Clements

LORD MAYOR

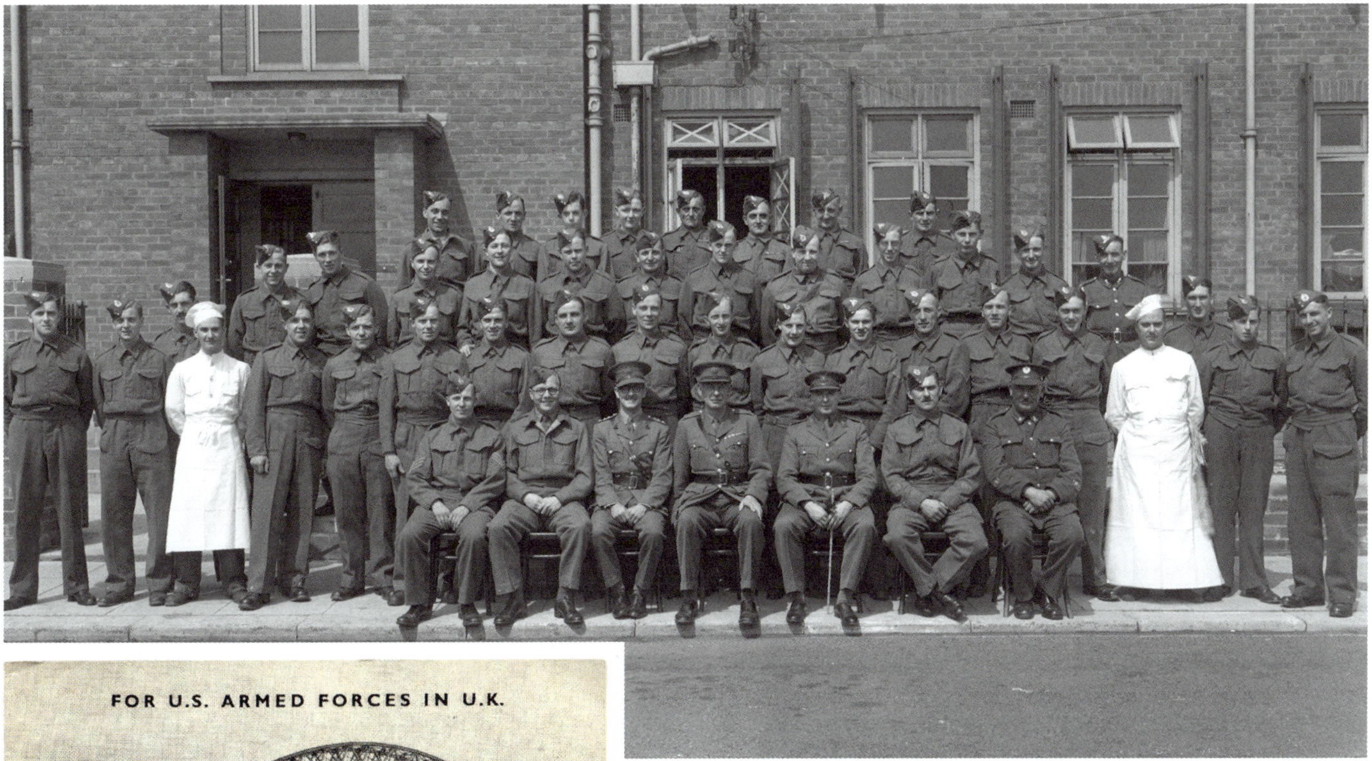

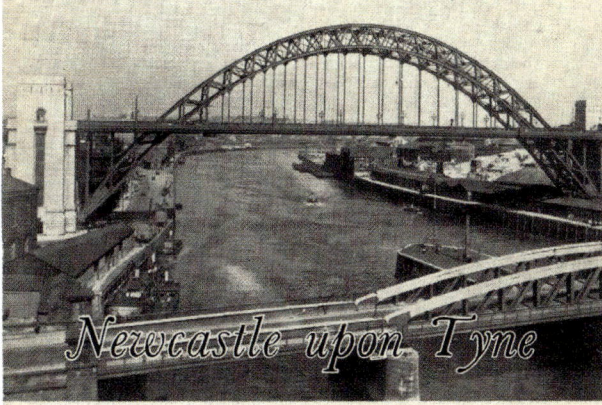

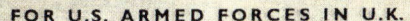

Above: Officers and men of 46th (Lincolnshire Regiment) Searchlight Regiment, at Debden Drill Hall, one of many AA units that helped defend Newcastle and Tyneside during the blitz of 1941. Left: Pocket guide to Newcastle produced for United States Armed Forces in the UK,1944.

THE MERCHANT NAVY

Men of the Merchant Navy photographed in Newcastle during the War

Many of the vessels that carried coal and other imports and exports the world over were built on the Tyne, brought back for refits and repairs to the Tyne and were often crewed, at least in part, by Tyneside lads. And during the war Newcastle provided safe harbour for vessels from many allied nations.

In 1939 Britain had the largest Merchant Navy in the world; vessels sailed under the Red Ensign otherwise known as the 'Red Duster' flag. Wartime voyages were fraught with danger as they sailed seas scattered with mines, faced attacks from U-boats and enemy aircraft, and braved storms. Merchant vessels were not used for military offensives but they were permitted to defend themselves with small arms if necessary and carried military personnel to operate the machine guns fitted to the vessels in wartime.

In 1939 Britain produced just one third of its food for home consumption; the rest was supplied from abroad. The losses of merchant vessels and the perilous journeys they faced slashed the amount of food imported to Britain and rationing was introduced in January 1940.

There are many stories of crew bravely fighting off attacks by enemy aircraft but there are also plenty of tragic tales of major losses. To illustrate the perils of serving in the Merchant Navy, here are just a couple of stories.

The first harks back to Dunkirk evacuation, when so many small merchant vessels and even pleasure craft answered the call to lend a hand. Former Felling Council employee, Merchant Seaman Robert Moody, was fireman aboard the *Levenwood* when she sailed for Dunkirk to bring troops home. When they approached harbour they found it was filled with smaller craft and they were unable to enter, so a call was made for volunteers to man the lifeboat and Moody and a number of the crew set off in the boat. Bombs were falling all around them, but they rowed on. Suddenly a big wave capsized their boat, pitching the crew into the water, but by some superhuman effort they managed to right it again. Fearing they may become grounded they stopped short of the shore. Moody, who was a strong and confident swimmer, dived over the side and swam to the stranded soldiers wading into the water. Moody went back and forth no less than ten times under a hail of fire from enemy planes. He carried non-swimmers on his back and helped others until the boat was full. Robert Moody was awarded a Distinguished Service Medal for his brave and selfless actions.

The Newcastle freighter SS *Carlton* had been bound for Buenos Aires, crossing the Atlantic some 430 miles off the West Coast of Ireland on 20 December 1940, when they spotted an enemy submarine. Crewman Amos Pearson recalled: *'The whole affair was like a nightmare. The submarine popped up alongside, not more than 12 yards away. We turned our gun on her (the Carlton was only armed with a Hotchkiss machine gun) but the bullets bounced off the hull like hailstones. She dived, but later we could see her periscope and she followed us all the morning.'*

Despite the best efforts of *Carlton's* captain to evade the sub by zig-zagging in the water they could not shake it off. At noon an enemy torpedo hit home and within six minutes the *Carlton* had sunk. All crew managed to scramble into the lifeboats, First Officer George Robinson of North Heaton launched one with 16 men and a further 17 were in a lifeboat with the captain. By nightfall the two lifeboats had separated and not long afterwards the captain's lifeboat capsized with the loss of all crew. Robinson's boat rowed and drifted, keeping an eye on the horizon for land or help for the next eighteen days when, at last, they were spotted and picked up by another merchant vessel. Robinson had ensured there was enough food to provide two biscuits and half a pint of fresh water each per day but as the days passed those supplied began to dwindle.

Bitterly cold winter winds and icy spray had lashed the lifeboat and one by one twelve members of the crew, including two lads aged just sixteen, died in front of their shipmates. As each man died he was buried at sea at night and First Officer Robinson read prayers for the dead. When they were finally picked up by another merchant vessel only Robinson and three others out of a total crew of 35 had survived. When they were brought in to an east Canadian port they were in a terrible state, suffering from frost bite and malnourished; they were described as 'little more than living skeletons.' Chief Officer George Robinson lost both his legs through exposure but he did make a recovery and was decorated with the OBE for his fortitude and leadership at Buckingham Palace in December 1942.

In an attempt to help guide shipping and provide better protection, merchant shipping often travelled in convoys under escort provided by Royal Navy vessels, notably the Arctic convoys that brought supplies from the UK, Iceland and North America to the Soviet Union ports such as Archangel and Murmansk between 1941 and 1945. In the latter years of the war there were between 2,000 and 3,000 British and Allied merchant ships at sea every day. Some 11.7 million tons of UK merchant shipping was lost and approximately 32,000 merchant seafarers were killed aboard convoy vessels between the years 1939-1945, which equated to a loss of 54 per cent of the total Merchant Navy fleet at the outbreak of the conflict.

It was claimed South Shields had a greater number of dry docks and repair facilities than any other town or city in the country. During a visit to South Shields in October 1944, Albert Victor Alexander, First Lord of the Admiralty paid tribute to local merchant seamen pointing out *'more sons of South Shields have paid the supreme sacrifice in service under the Red Ensign than from any other town in the country.'*

SS Shahristan, built at Redhead's, South Shields, in 1938 and sunk off the Azores by U-371 on 30 July 1941 with the loss of the ship's master, 38 crew and 26 passengers

Sadly the identity of the members of the Merchant Navy on these photographs has not been recorded. All that is known is the photographs were taken in Newcastle during the Second World War. We publish them in a tribute to all forgotten heroes.

A snapshot of the crew of a Royal Navy Arctic convoy escort on an iced up deck of their ship c1942

THE HOME GUARD

Gosforth Home Guard marching to a film show at the Regency Cinema, 21 April 1941

After seven months of the 'Phoney War', the Battle of France began in earnest on 10 May 1940. Hitler had unleashed his blitzkrieg and German forces sped through the continent with apparent ease. The fall of Belgium, France and Holland left many in no doubt that Britain would face the onslaught next. Particular concerns were expressed in both the local and national newspapers over the use of German paratroops being dropped in advance of any invasion.

Local Invasion committees were formed and groups of men and women gathered together to discuss how they would defend their homes. They formed irregular units and began patrolling country areas after dark armed with shotguns. Riders with local hunts were slinging sporting rifles and slipping handguns into their saddlebags. Government and military authorities were uncomfortable with the idea of unregulated partisan bands forming around the country so it was suggested that if such martial enthusiasm was organized properly

'Parachutes Over Britain' by John Langdon Davies (1940) suggested ways to observe and deal with the parachute menace

on a town and village basis into a volunteer defence force it could provide a valuable counter measure against the parachute menace. As the morning papers of 14 May carried headlines of a 2,000-tank clash north of Liege, bundles of enrolment forms began to arrive at police stations and it was made known an important announcement would be made on the BBC Home Service that evening. Just after 9.00pm on 14 May 1940, Anthony Eden, the newly appointed Home Secretary, made the appeal for men not in military service between the ages of 17 and 65 to come forward and offer their services in a new force to be known as the Local Defence Volunteers (LDV).

Local Defence Volunteers were asked to enrol at the local police station and many men set off to join immediately. Some volunteers arrived at police stations even before the broadcast had ended, setting out with the intention of being the very first to volunteer, only to find a queue had already formed in front of them. Many of them turned up in their work clothes, bank clerks in smart suits, bus drivers in their uniforms and workmen in their overalls. The announcement had been like a pistol shot at the start of a race and the volunteers poured in, not in hundreds as anticipated but in their thousands through the night and following day. Nationally some 250,000 gave their names in the first 24 hours.

So rapid was the response that the enrolment forms had not reached every police station, but police officers amicably took down names and addresses. It was days before the official forms reached either Newcastle or Gateshead, so simple forms were devised and printed on duplicating machines giving instructions that each volunteer was to be asked: Your name and address. Are you familiar with firearms? Your occupation? What military experience have you? Are you prepared to serve away from home? The policemen involved with the enrolments were also given clear instructions that they were not concerned with the administration or control of the LDVs, only the registering of the names and addresses of volunteers. They were advised to exercise discretion by 'politely sending away' and not recording the names of those clearly too young or too infirm.

Prior to Eden's broadcast the Lord Lieutenants of every county were sent a telegram from the Home Secretary requesting their help with the establishment of the LDV by appointing an Area Commander with overall command and organisational responsibility for the county. Each county was divided into zones based on existing police division areas. In each zone a headquarters was established to administer the number of groups within it. Brevet Colonel Viscount Allendale MC was appointed County Commandant for Northumberland.

The Northumberland Groups and their Commanders were:

Berwick: Capt. The Hon. Claud Lambton DSO
Alnwick: Lieut-Col. The Hon. H G O Bridgeman DSO, MC
Morpeth: Colonel B. Cruddas, DSO, MP
Hexham: Lieut-Col. Sir Archibald White
Gosforth: Brigadier-General J. Greene DSO
Blyth: Major E H Watson TD
Wallsend: Mr J Hall
Tynemouth: Mr Stanley Holmes

Local solicitor Colonel George F. Bell, who had served as a Captain in 6th Battalion, Northumberland Fusiliers during the First World War and commanded the battalion from 1932-36 was appointed the Newcastle Group Commander with Captain Tommy Sopwith, Second in Command. 3,000 men had applied for enrolment in the city, but with only four companies allotted the numbers that could be accepted were limited and initially only 250 men were required for what the media often referred to as 'the parashots' in those early days.

The numbers involved were not quite like the army: where a regular army platoon consists of 30 men the LDV equivalent could range between ten and 50 men. Most of those appointed to command positions in the LDV had previous military experience but it was not essential as those with respected managerial, organizational and leadership skills from civvy street also found themselves in positions of command. In those early days when numbers were restricted, a number of the bigger local companies also raised their own LDV units for factory defence. There were also LDV units on the railways and at the Post Office. As ever it was the best men for the job of leadership and there were several instances of bosses proudly falling in with all ranks of the LDV.

Much to the chagrin of many suitable volunteers already serving in the ARP or in the Special Constabulary, they had to be turned down in case the forces they had already been trained in became too depleted. In reality the recruitment terms were flexible, in some small villages men served as both Home Guards (HG) and ARP or the HG platoon had an ARP duties section. Discretion was shown towards old soldiers, especially ex-NCOs over the age limit, who had valuable experience to impart if they were apparently fit enough.

For all those disappointed not to have been able to join the LDV and those wishing to get a bit of drill and fitness training under their belts, very much in the spirit of the Newcastle Citizens Training Corps that was raised in 1914, Newcastle began a Voluntary Training Corps for all ages. Drill was taught, the men marched, had physical training and played in sports matches. Based at St. James's Park and backed by the Lord Mayor, famous footballers like Stan Seymour and Andy McCombie urged others to join and helped with the training.

The duties of the Local Defence Volunteers were threefold. First and foremost it was for observation, to spot paratroops or invasion forces and report back. These duties gave rise to the nickname of the unit – 'Look, Duck and Vanish.' Secondly, they should help stop the free movement of any invading enemy by blocking railway lines and immobilising cars and other motorised vehicles. Thirdly, they were to patrol 'vulnerable spots' such as railway bridges, gas, electricity and water works to prevent sabotage.

Initially they were just issued armbands made from khaki material bearing the letters LDV. Uniforms of denim battledress blouses and trousers worn with side hats followed soon after. Supplies were limited so some men were left waiting a few weeks until their uniforms arrived. As British forces massed on the beaches of Dunkirk in late May 1940, Newcastle's churches had some of their largest congregations in living memory and as signage and direction posts were obliterated or taken down across the county thoughts and fears were raised of what may happen next. The arming of the LDV was now a matter for concern. There was a limited supply of training rifles, a few arms of Great War and earlier vintage were pressed into service, but many units were reduced to learning drill with broomsticks and the few shotguns the members of their platoon already had. Consequently a number of the local papers published appeals for 12-bore cartridges to be handed in to police station so they may be distributed to LDV units.

On 14 June notifications appeared in newspapers and on posters stating the ringing of church bells had been prohibited and that they would only be rung by military authorities or members of the LDV to warn the public of parachutists or airborne troops approaching. An appeal was also made for members of the public not to make pleasure trips to parts of the East Coast. These applied to an area spreading from the Wash to Sussex, but it was expanded to include much of the coast in an unbroken line up to Berwick on Tweed soon after. The Honourable Member for Consett, Mr David Adams went so far as to suggest to the Minister of Health in the House of Commons that there should be a compulsory evacuation of Tyneside. Mr Adams was referred to Registration figures that suggested parents would not be likely to co-operate with such a scheme. In fact, a vote at the Newcastle Education Committee on whether or not to evacuate 10,000 children from the city was only supported by three votes. Hitler was not going to shift the Geordies!

As ever, the letters pages of newspapers provide some remarkable insights into the thoughts and opinions of people at the time. In June 1940, as the fear of invasion intensified, the *Newcastle Weekly Chronicle* included a letter to the editor from a correspondent identified by their initials M.P., of Windy Nook that showed an uncanny premonition of the scenario that Jack Higgins employed in his book *The Eagle Has Landed* (1975):

Sir,
This is a Christian and charitable land. One of the oldest Christian and charitable customs, handed down from times when churches were sanctuaries in the very literal sense, is the custom of leaving our church doors always unlocked, by night as well as by day.

In these days when the parachutist menace is in everyone's mind, is this wise? To a parachutist landing by night and possibly unobserved the open church would afford temporary hiding, a few hours' sleep and a place to change in. He might even indulge in a little looting should he feel so inclined!

I think all churches should be locked by night for the duration of the war.

As the LDV found its feet and regular patrols were undertaken, they too encountered a few suspicious characters or those who just had not realised how far the war emergency restrictions had been taken. In one instance a North Gosforth Reverend was seen taking a photograph of a Northumberland harbour. Innocent enough in peace time, but this was war. He was spotted by a LDV who requested he hand over the reel of film and he ended up in court where he was fined £2 and 12 shillings costs. A number of other individuals were brought before the magistrates and fined after failing to

Dicky Douglas (77) shows great interest in the rifle shown to him by John Tough, a fisherman turned Home Guard on Holy Island, 1942

produce their identity cards when sentries and patrols required then to do so.

On 23 July 1940 Winston Churchill, who had never liked the cumbersome and somewhat ridiculed title of Local Defence Volunteers, formally announced that the organization be re-named Home Guard. This also ushered in a raft of improvements, structured training, uniform and weaponry supplies and official recognition were set in motion for HG units across the country.

Churchill also appealed to the United States for the first major issue of rifles for HGs. His call was answered with a batch of Canadian Ross rifles and, by far the larger issue of half a million P.14 and P.17 Springfield rifles, all of First World War vintage. These came in thick paraffin grease and many platoon histories record the sterling work of women volunteers including local WVS, who helped to clean the weapons, but ammunition and cleaning materials for rifle maintenance were still in short supply.

A training school for Home Guards had been established in the grounds of Osterley Park, Hounslow, West London. Its Director was Tom Wintringham, who had commanded the British Battalion of the International Brigade during the Spanish Civil War. He, along with his team of experts, trained Home Guards in the methods of guerilla warfare to be deployed against potential invasion forces. The first selected men from units in Northumberland attended a two-day course in guerilla fighting and tank destruction there in July 1940.

Concerns over enemy parachutists were ever present in newspapers and magazines and the military correspondent of the *Weekly Chronicle* wrote a special article entitled *Do This and Upset Parachutists* in which it was suggested:

> *"Suspect any man who calls at your house and asks for maps, about means of transport or anything like that. Refuse any information and as soon as he is gone, get in touch with the police. If you are a Home Guard or an armed soldier, insist that the stranger puts his hands up and accompanies you to the nearest police station...Don't be afraid. The parachutists are probably a lot more scared than you could ever be."*

Trying to ignore the wartime restrictions, could have fatal consequences. At one incident at East Howdon in September 1940, a Home Guard challenged a man he had seen lurking with a woman in shadows. It was dark and the Home Guard told the man he would have to accompany him down the road to have a look at his identity card. As they walked the man stopped on more than one occasion and said 'If only you had not your rifle.' This attitude worried the Home Guard. He called for assistance but the man made a lunge towards him as if to take the rifle off him. The Home Guard fired what he intended as a warning shot but it hit the man and he was taken to Tynemouth infirmary where he later died from the wound. At the Inquest the Coroner warned: *'the general public should be careful to recognise the protection they were getting by means of the Home Guard and that they should take care what they did when challenged.'*

The Home Guard maintained their dusk-till-dawn patrols long after the immediate threat of invasion had passed. Many of these men would then have to go and do a day's work although many of the retired 'old boys' took the dawn watch so the younger working men could get a good night's sleep. As the war progressed many of the younger lads came of age for call up and more recruits, usually those just below that age, would take their place. There never seemed to be a problem with recruitment for the Home Guard in Newcastle and it could even claim a few remarkable members, among them the man believed to be the shortest Home Guard in the country, Monty Pearson (16) a jockey from Lemington, who served with a section of fellow jockeys nicknamed 'The Tichies.' The other was one of the youngest to enrol as a fully-fledged member of the Home Guard; Ronald Robson, aged just 14, who was accepted for service with a new platoon based in St Barnabas Church Hall.

After a slow start, when most Home Guard armouries consisted of training rifles and petrol bombs known as 'Molotov Cocktails', the situation changed over the months until most Home Guard Companies had quite an array of weapons. There were bayonets for their rifles, Thompson sub-machine guns, Browning automatic rifles appeared in most platoons and

Army Cadet Force Detachment, Heaton, June 1942. The Army Cadet Force was ideal for both working with the Home Guard and for training young men for military service. Below: Officers and NCOs of Willington Quay Company, 8th Battalion, Northumberland Home Guard outside Willington Parish Hall, 2 December 1943

Members of Northumberland Home Guard marching past the South African War Memorial at Barras Bridge, Newcastle, where the salute was taken at their 'stand down' parade, 3 December 1944

companies often had the likes of Lewis or Vickers machine guns. Thompsons were later recalled from HG units and issued to commandos; the gap in the HG armoury was later filled by an issue of Sten guns. The first weapon received by anti-tank sections was The Blacker Bombard (later retitled Spigot Mortar). This was a cumbersome weapon; the three man crew could deploy the weapon to be fired from the ground on its potable mountings or mounted on one of the many concreted spigot mortar mount emplacements fixed at defensive points across the county. Anti-tank sections were much happier with the arrival of Northover Projectors, designed by Major Robert Harry Northover, specifically for use by the Home Guard. There was also the Smith Gun. Mounted on a light gun carriage, it could be towed behind a car and upended for deployment. The idea was good, but it was prone to explode and claimed the lives of a number of Home Guards around the country.

As Hitler turned his attention to the Russian Front and his aspirations for an invasion of Britain faded further and further away, Britain's Home Guard kept sharp with regular training that was put to the test in large-scale exercises. The mock invasion exercise in September 1942 involved Home Guard units, Regular Army and

Civil Defence Services from Newcastle and Tyneside. The 'enemy' troops, played by the Regulars, made good ground over the 10-hour exercise, but a senior officer criticised reports in some newspapers that claimed the Home Guard had been annihilated, commenting: *'If the enemy did reach their objectives it does not signify they captured Newcastle. Thousands of defenders were still available to deal with the situation. Although decisions were given in their favour, it is probable that many of the 'invaders' who reached the centre of the city would never have done so if it had been the real thing'.* He went on to point out he had complete confidence in the ability of the Home Guard to hold an invasion of much greater numbers than fielded for the exercise.

As artillerymen were deployed abroad, Home Guard units gradually took over the manning of Anti-Aircraft Batteries and the first 'kill' by a HG crew was credited to 110 Battery on Tyneside in 1942. The new 'Z' Rocket Batteries and some Heavy AA battery duties were also passed to Home Guard units and artillery gunners were replaced along the coast at many locations with 'emergency batteries' manned by Home Guard from October 1942. After the successful progress of the Allies after the D-Day landings in June 1944, the need for the Home Guard rapidly diminished. On 30 August 1944 the War Office issued Instructions for Standing Down the Home Guard and a formal notice circulated in October gave notification that it was to stand down from active duties in November 1944.

On 3 December 1944 thousands of members of Northumberland Home Guard took part in their 'stand down' parades. Some went down to London to represent Northumberland in a grand march past the King. In Newcastle more than 3,000 representatives of all units in Northumberland, with four bands in attendance, marched from Newcastle Central Station to the South African War Memorial at Barras Bridge, where the salute was taken by the District Commander, Major General A E Robinson. The Home Guardsmen

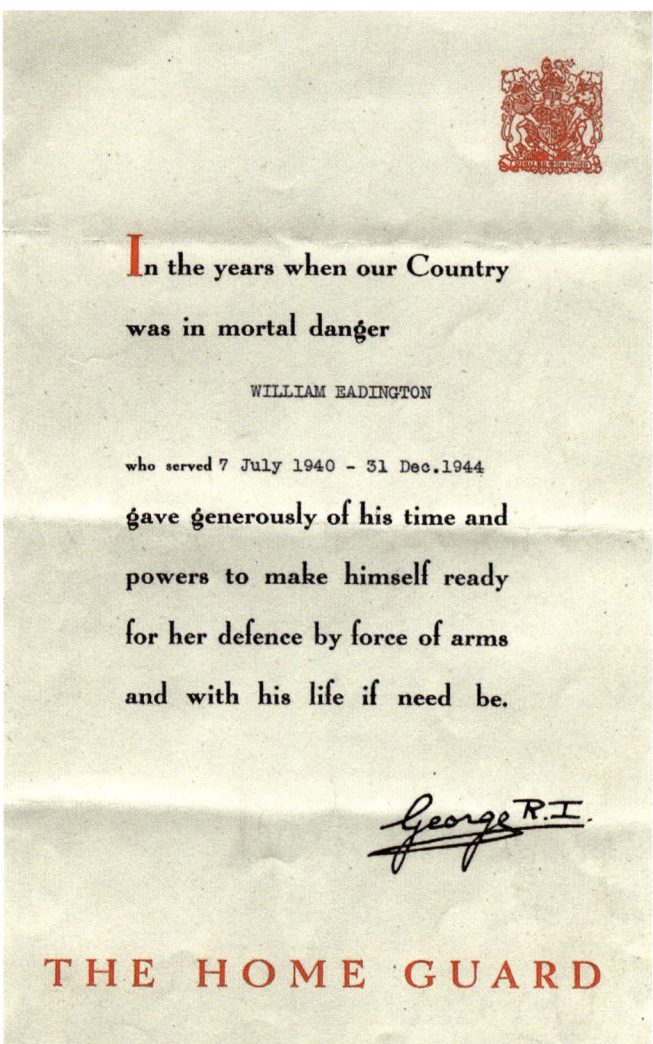

Home Guard service certificate presented to William Eadington, Pit Deputy at Isabella Pit, Blyth, a stalwart of 6th Battalion, Northumberland Home Guard

on parade assembled in the Haymarket Cinema and the Palace Theatre, where they were formally, but nonetheless sincerely, thanked for the great service they rendered in the country's darkest hours.

Auxiliary Units

Auxiliary Units, sometimes referred to as 'Churchill's Secret Army,' were part of a top secret organization whose members, in the event of invasion, were to go to ground, allow the enemy to pass over, and then rise up in as a resistance army to harry the army of occupation. Only part of the Home Guard (HG) for administrative purposes, the Auxiliaries organization drew on HG membership to hand pick men for its special duties and even adopted HG uniforms to cloak its members occasional appearances on manoeuvres.

Devised by guerilla warfare expert Major Colin McVean Gubbins, the man who would go on to mastermind the Special Operations Executive, a letter from the offices of the War Cabinet outlined:

These Auxiliary Units are being formed with two objectives:

'A) They are intended to provide, within the framework of the Home Guard organization, small bodies of men especially selected and trained, whose role it will be to act offensively on the flanks and in the rear of any enemy troops who may obtain a foothold in this country. Their action will particularly directed against tanks and lorries ... ammunition dumps, small enemy posts and stragglers. Their activities will also include sniping.

B) The other function of the Auxiliary Units is to provide a system of intelligence whereby Regular Forces in the field can be kept informed of what is happening behind enemy lines.'

The letter went on to point out that each unit would comprise no more than a dozen men, they were to be provided with weaponry and equipped with wireless and field telephones apparatus. Each unit was to be accommodated in specially-designed camouflaged and concealed (usually underground) operational bases (OBs) where food, water, weapons and ammunition

Wartime training aid booklet for fighting patrols c1941

would be stored. Once training got underway, the Auxiliaries were also taught how to disrupt enemy railways by blowing up tracks, how to destroy petrol and ammunition dumps and how to immobilize enemy aircraft on occupied airfields.

In practice the objective 'A' Auxiliary Units were to become known as Operational Patrols and usually comprised of between four to eight men in each unit. Patrols would only operate in an area within 15 miles of their base. In the event of a successful invasion and enemy occupation they were not to communicate in any way with army command, they had to be isolated and autonomous until a successful counter attack was made

Battledress sleeve insignia worn by members of Northumberland Auxiliary units when in uniform.

or they were wiped out. All Auxiliaries were warned that their operational life expectancy, if there was an invasion, was about two weeks, if they were lucky.

Objective 'B' units became known as Special Duties Section and Signals. These units contained both men and women who were trained to identify vehicles, high-ranking officers and military units, and were to gather intelligence and leave reports in dead letter drops. The reports would be collected by runners and taken to one of over 200 secret radio transmitters operated by trained civilian signals staff.

Gubbins began his recruitment drive with a team of twelve hand-picked intelligence officers. Every man who was to serve in the Auxiliary Units had to be very carefully selected.

The first Intelligence Officer (IO) for Northumberland and the Scottish borders was Captain James 'Hamish' Watt-Torrance, appointed early in 1940. He scouted out sites for the first OBs, organised their construction by Royal Engineers (local contractors could not be trusted to keep the secret) and identified and contacted the right men to become his group commanders to establish the Auxiliary Units in the county. Watt-Torrance moved on in 1941 and his work was carried on by Captain Anthony Quayle, a man who went on to international fame in the post-war years as an actor in such films as *The Guns of Navarone*. Looking back on his time as IO for Northumberland years later, Quayle recalled how impressed he was by the commitment and skills demonstrated by the patrols and, even though he went on to see active service in Albania, he maintained the men of the Northumberland patrols demonstrated some of the finest field craft skills he had ever seen.

Once the group commanders were recruited, they in turn would seek out about nine men to operate each of their patrols, one of whom would be appointed patrol leader. They would all have to sign the Official Secrets Act and would be sent to Coleshill House for their training in unarmed combat, explosives, weapons handing and fieldcraft. Local training centres for Auxiliary units with tough Norwegian instructors were established in the county at Alnwick and Shielow Castle, north of Belford. The members of the patrols came from a huge variety of backgrounds from miners, farm labourers and gamekeepers, to bank managers, farmers, doctors and local council officials from teens up to those in their seventies.

In Northumberland the northern group commander was Scremerston farmer Lambert Carmichael; his brother Alan ran another group for the Morpeth area. Peter Robinson commanded at Seahouses and his brother Robert Robinson's group covered the Alnwick area. Among Robinson's men was Peter Robson, an Alnwick mole catcher, who, despite having just one arm, was a true marksman who knew the value of patience and the cover of darkness well. He knew the countryside around his home intimately. Those who served with Robson would recall: 'he would have gone through his entire life happily killing a German a day.' Then there was the redoubtable bank manager Robert 'Bob' Hall, who led the Bedlington group, which operated out of cleverly hidden underground bunkers in woodland near Bedlington, Chevington, Stobswood, Ellington and Cramlington. Bob would recall decades later:

'I had a splendid bunch of chaps — mostly all pitmen- even today I regard them as the salt of the earth. Frankly, I recruited them on unusual grounds. I liked to hear of troublemakers, rabblerousers and fighters or the chaps who obviously wanted excitement'.

No wonder they got the reputation and nickname of the 'Death or Glory Boys.' Units of trained civilians they might have been, but many of these lads also took their turn on duty up at Balmoral as the personal bodyguard for the Royal Family when they were in residence. Many Auxiliary Unit members had no uniforms and performed their duties in their work clothes or perhaps a set of army denims and a cap comforter, but those on duty at Balmoral were issued with battledress bearing the insignia of the 'Home Guard' shoulder title, the county patch and below that the number 201, the unique HG unit number of auxiliary units in Scotland, Northumberland and the northernmost counties of England.

Their one common bond was they had the ability, above all, to keep a secret, they could not even tell their wives because, if invasion came and they were interrogated, they would have nothing to tell. Some of them were stigmatised by their local communities for not appearing to be 'doing their bit' for the war effort and many veterans of the Auxiliary Units waited decades after the war to reveal the truth about their wartime activities to their families. Even today their caches of weaponry and explosives or previously unknowns OBs posts are found quite by chance in the woodlands of Northumberland, but there is little else to remind us of these men who would have defended our country to the last ditch, the last man and the last round but then as they would say, secrecy was the name of their game.

Lapel badge presented to members of Auxiliary units after their stand down in 1945

ALIENS AND SPIES

Public vigilance was encouraged in all media from dramatic films to stories in the press throughout the war to consider if the people around us, especially strangers, were friend or foe?

The status of Newcastle and Tyneside as one of Britain's most important centres for armament production, coal mining, shipyards, engineering, Royal Navy facilities and merchant shipping was only too well known to Britain's intelligence community in the 1930s. The area attracted the attention of fascist and socialist groups, certain individuals identified as 'subversive' and, perhaps, even more disconcerting, the German businessmen and reporters that visited and took more than a passing interest in the important industries of the area. Among them was Rolf Hoffmann, head of the Nazi German Government Foreign Press Department

Luftwaffe target map of Newcastle, 1939

who, during one such visit to the North East in March 1938, gave an interview to the *Sunderland Echo* in which he explained he liked to visit England as often as he could to make 'contacts for the encouragement of better relationships between Germany and Britain'. He took pains to point out:

'The Englishman is fair, but it is unfortunate some people believe that German people are maintained under some sort of suppression. Nothing is further from the truth.'

Visits such as Hoffman's and the activities of political groups of the extreme left and right wings attracted the attention of local Special Branch and police detectives and in the early 1930s MI5 considered it prudent to open a local office in Newcastle. There were a few such offices around the country, each one was a closely guarded secret and correspondence sent between the local authorities and the various MI5 offices would always simply be addressed to Box 500, Newcastle or Box 500, Oxford and so on.

In the days before the internet and mobile phones it was far easier to monitor the communications of a person of interest. They could be followed and watched and if a Home Office Warrant or 'HOW' was obtained, their telephone calls could be listened to and recorded and their post intercepted, opened, copied for later scrutiny, resealed and sent on to the addressee. Just such an operation was carried out in the 'Home Office Room' at Newcastle's postal sorting office at Orchard Street.

Such was the hatred of Hitler and the Nazis that even those who had fled to Britain to escape the Nazi heel could be suspected of being Nazi collaborators who had come over to Britain to merge into British society, only to spy on the British defences and important military installations and even commit acts of sabotage and co-operation if the enemy invasion had taken place. Suspicions like these had rumbled around in Britain from the mid 1930s; those suspected of being collaborators were labelled 'Fifth Columnists' (a term originated by General Emilio Mola for internal collaborators during the Spanish Civil War) and a climate of fear and concern over the suspected growth of the shadowy fifth column reached fever pitch as the British army retreated to Dunkirk and invasion scares intensified.

Under Defence Regulation 18b, all 'aliens' had to register with local authorities from the outset of the war. In May 1940 all 'enemy aliens' (all those of German or Austrian nationality) between the age of sixteen and sixty that were living in a number of areas along the east and south east coast of Britain were to be rounded up and interned, all 'aliens' (anyone other than a British citizen) had their movements restricted, specifically:

1. They should report daily in person to a police station
2. They shall not make any use of a motor vehicle (other than a public conveyance) or any bicycle
3. They shall not be out of doors between the hours of 8.00pm and 6.00am

They were also forbidden to have in their possession a camera, film camera, sketch book, wireless transmitter, telescope, binoculars, nautical charts or maps. Restrictions were also applied to one of the great Northern passions of the day – racing pigeons. As they could be used to carry messages for spies, anyone wishing to keep a pigeon loft had to obtain the necessary permit and those who did not would face prosecution and having their birds destroyed.

The 18b regulations were applied with rigour but they had not dealt with British citizens in pro-Nazi or Fascist organisations and members of these organisations were also arrested and imprisoned or interned. When the 18b regulations were extended to Northumberland in early June 1940, over fifty men were detained in Newcastle and around 300 non-German 'aliens' were required to comply with the restriction order. Within days the knock on the door came for Italians living in Newcastle, about a dozen were interned immediately and others were subject to the strictest curfew regulations.

Lists of those who might be considered as potential collaborators, often based on them having worked in Germany before the war or having been known to have expressed pro-German opinions, were also drawn up by Chief Constables and Special Branch and submitted to the Home Office. A 'Suspect List' was made of those who should be watched or noted for future reference and was maintained throughout the war.

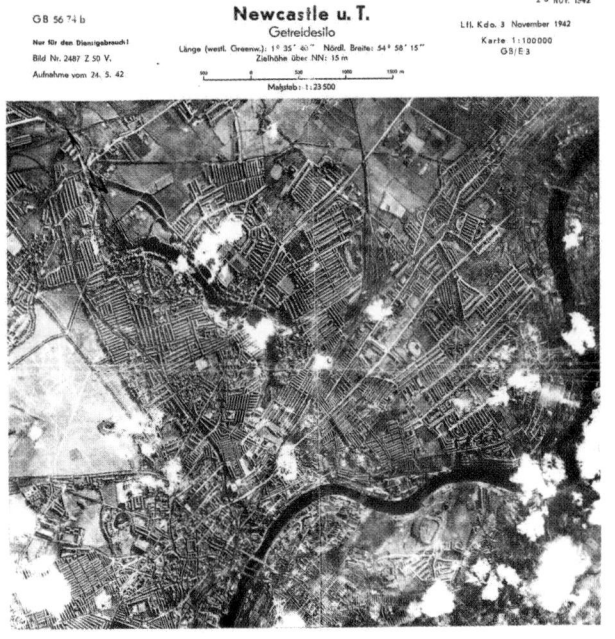

Luftwaffe aerial reconnaissance photograph of Newcastle, November 1942

Those who were interned were initially held in prisons or detention centres in Britain and were then moved to detention camps, many of them converted from old hotels, on the Isle of Man. The order was later extended to women, who would be permitted to take their children with them if they were interned. Many would spend months or even years behind barbed wire as tribunals sat and those who were judged 'of least concern' were gradually released.

Even after the internments, the fear remained that a Fifth Column was now operating underground and spies were being landed by parachute or from rubber dinghies. False alarms were rife and the police and Home Guard were kept on their toes with mistaken sightings and suspicious characters. Clouds in the moonlight, puffs of smoke discharged from the barrels of AA guns and the reflected light of a searchlight off a barrage balloon were some of the causes of supposed sightings of enemy parachutists. Scares over Fifth Columnists were often rumour based, for example malicious stories spread about someone shining a torch to guide enemy aircraft to their target. The mysterious noise of scrabbling of feet over rooftops in August 1940 also led to concerns of Fifth Columnists at work in the Ocean Road area of South Shields. The police were notified but on investigation the culprit turned out to be a pet monkey named Jacko. He had escaped and his master had been called to sea without having the chance to recover his pet. The distressed animal began screaming at night, people complained they could not sleep and the monkey was eventually shot down from his rooftop perch by a policeman.

Hand in hand with stories of suspected Fifth Columnists went stories of suspected spies although many were found to be false. During the war some spies were landed in Britain and, as once-secret files have been released, more has been found out about them. Some were executed, some turned double agent, others got away with it. Among them was a spy who operated out of Whitley Bay; he was hardly George Smiley, but he was far from fictional.

An MI5 file, now declassified and accessible to the public via The National Archives, reveals that one Gerrit Schut, aka Johann Schutt, Johann Peulen or Peuylen, was born in Rotterdam in 1917 (neither his true name nor his origins are clear) and appears to have been recruited by German intelligence in the late 1930s. He made the first of his known regular trips to Britain in January 1939. Schut described himself variously as a ship's chandler, a ship-buying agent for Holland, a bulb grower and a diamond merchant. He began in Glasgow, where he spoke freely in the hotel he was staying about his late father's shipping business that he had inherited. He claimed he had come to this country to buy ships. On several occasions he was found to be telling lies. On one occasion he stated that he had bought a particular ship on the Clyde, but unbeknown to Schut a ship's captain was residing in the hotel where he was staying at the time. Schut was standing drinks all round that night, celebrating the alleged purchase of the ship. The captain enquired about the purchase the following day learned that the vessel had not been sold.

Schut left soon afterwards and did not return to the Clyde but he moved his operations to Whitley Bay. His methods changed little, he represented himself as a Dutch broker for a Rotterdam shipping company and often had money to buy drinks and celebrate the success of his business deals with others in the bars where he had become known, specifically at the Rex Hotel and the Esplanade Hotel at Whitley Bay and the Park Hotel, Tynemouth.

It appears he made a lot of contacts, but little bore fruit. He was known to have made the acquaintance of two of the beach photographers, but they were not willing to comply with his requests for photographs of the guns at Tynemouth Castle. At Whitley Bay Schut had been seen with an expensive Leica camera with a special lens. On another occasion, while at the Rex, his cover was almost blown when a well-meaning member of hotel staff introduced Schut to a Dutch lady, Miss Geraldine Franken. Miss Franken was left with the impression Schut was not Dutch at all because he spoke so badly and she thought he sounded more like a German. The police and MI5 were aware of Schut and some of those he was tying to recruit from late 1939, but having been highly delighted to have successfully uncovered a spy operating in the North they had been very disappointed to discover that he had already left and did not follow up on his known associates. In fairness to MI5, their resources were already stretched as they investigated hundreds of cases of suspected spies, Fifth Columnists and other suspicious individuals.

In May 1940 Schut was arrested in Holland as a suspected enemy agent. He had maps of gun emplacements from the North-East coast of England and his papers revealed he was in touch with two individuals in particular. MI5 was contacted at 'Box 500', Newcastle, where the case was assigned to Major C P Hope to liaise with local police and investigate further. One of those named was a 33-year-old Sunderland widow whom he met at a dance at The Park Hotel in Tynemouth in May 1939. The general impression among Schut's associates at Whitley Bay was that Schut and the widow were to marry. Investigations revealed she worked at a Sunderland radio retailer and was known to go out every Tuesday, returning late each time. It was also known that she received occasional post from Holland and Norway. One day she was followed by a Special Branch officer and the people she visited were checked. All were found to be of good standing and not known to have any connections to pro-German organisations but the police left a note on her file stating that they considered her 'a loose woman.' On 14 May 1940 her house was searched and she was brought in for an interview conducted by Sunderland Police. She was asked whether she had any correspondence in her possession regarding friendships with foreign seamen. Without hesitation she stated that she had various letters and telegrams from a Dutchman named Gerrit Schut, who she believed to be a ship's broker from Rotterdam.

She stated that she had met him at a dance held in the Queen's Hotel, Whitley Bay about May 1939. Since that time she had corresponded with him on various occasions and had spent the week prior to the outbreak of war in 1939 with him at the Zuid-Hollandsch Hotel, Rotterdam, returning to England on the day war was declared. Whilst there she had met a woman who was

The Rex Hotel, Whitley Bay, one of the recruiting grounds for spies for Germany in 1939. Below: The Park Hotel, Tynemouth where enemy agent Gerrit Schut picked up a number of local female 'contacts' in 1939

introduced as his sister. Schut had proposed marriage to her but she had not treated the matter seriously. She stated that he had never at any time asked any questions regarding shipping, nor had she supplied him with any information of this nature. Between May and August 1939 she met him about four times in Whitley Bay, once in Hull and once in Sunderland on the occasion when he came to take her to Holland.

Schut's other contact was a man from Whitley Bay. He was a former Territorial soldier who had served in the First World War. After the war he had returned to his old employment in the GPO SC & T (Sorting, Counting, Telegraphs and Telephones) and stayed there for years, but having hit hard times and with a family to support he turned to theft. He was caught stealing postal packets and had received a custodial sentence with hard labour in 1932. Dismissed from his former job, he had found it very hard to find work and had taken occasional work as a bookie's runner. He had become a salaried ARP warden on the outbreak of war. Brought in for interview, he confirmed he had paid regular visits to the Esplanade Hotel, Whitley Bay when he was working as a bookie's runner. He asked the manager if he had any work going there on a number of occasions and the manager introduced him to Gerrit Schut. The man recalled that Schut did not speak English particularly well 'passable like but not perfect by any means.' He had his suspicions about the man but he desperately needed money and asked Schut if he could get him a job. Schut invited him over to Rotterdam to see if they could find him some work. While over in Holland:

'he [Schut] was so evasive in many ways, and never told me what the job was going to be until just on our return journey ... he told me he wanted some information on shipbuilding and things like that. He said it was because it was in his line and that I would help him in his work. I honestly did not really believe him.'

Schut gave him £40, including £20 for his travelling expenses for the Holland trip, and he was left with about £20 in pocket. He admitted that he had been sure that Schut was a German agent but claimed he knew very little about his activities and that what information he had supplied was obtained from a book that was available to the general public across Europe. The visits occurred twice more, on the next he even met Schut's boss, a man introduced as Captain Johnson at Hotel Atlantic. His English was also very poor. His last visit was in August 1939 and he returned eight days before war broke out. Each time he carried letters through customs back to England where he bought stamps and posted them from South Shields, possibly to other duped individuals who could then pass them to their contacts who they may or may not have realised were spies, all in an effort to avoid interception while they were being handled by the GPO.

By this time Schut was long gone and was soon released from custody after the German occupation of Holland. According to his MI5 file he was believed to be living in Paris and was thought to have been involved in plots to get individuals to plant explosives on allied merchant shipping. He was not spotted again until 1943 when he was seen in Spain with another Nazi businessman-cum-agent and was seen entering Spain from Gibraltar on a number of subsequent occasions. In 1943. Gibraltar was a highly sensitive place, key to allied shipping in the Mediterranean during the war, and there is no way Schut should have been allowed there, but it is intriguing to note that the man responsible for counter-intelligence in the area at the time was a certain Harold 'Kim' Philby, who was revealed as a double agent before defecting to the Soviet Union in 1963.

Meanwhile, back in the North East Schut's female acquaintance was kept under observation by the police and a local informer. The male accomplice was arrested under article 18b and detained until November 1943 when he was released under restrictions, it being felt German Intelligence Service would approach him again. However, subsequent notes in his MI5 file show he was indeed contacted by foreign intelligence agency operatives after the end of the war.

We know very little more at the moment, but it seems there is more to tell; writing on the case in October 1940 Captain Derek Tangye of MI5 wrote in reply to an enquiry from Newcastle Box 500:

'Indeed I wish I had never heard the name of Schut. As soon as I have time I will write you a book on him and all his associates, together with a description of his relations with Miss XXXX. At the moment the files are 'lost'...'

Who knows what will be released and revealed in the future?

WOMEN WAR WORKERS

Joan Brown (Second right on back row) with her pals from the wages department of Vickers Armstrongs at Riding Mill, Tyne Valley c1941

Women of Tyneside and Northumberland served in a host of civilian wartime organisations throughout the Second World War such as the British Red Cross Society and Order of St John, Civil Nursing Reserve, YMCA, YWCA and NAAFI; some of them also served abroad with these units. One of the most remarkable local war workers was 80-year-old mother of 22, Mrs Estella Miller of Brock Street, Byker. Her service history dated back to the Zulu War when she was a nurse, a duty she also performed during the South African War (1899-1902) when she was caught in in the sieges of Ladysmith and Mafeking. When the First World War broke out she volunteered to nurse wounded soldiers again. In the Second World War she busied herself knitting socks and comforts but that was not enough for this lady of action and she offered her services to the Newcastle Royal Infirmary. Sadly her eyesight was failing and hospital authorities had to decline her offer.

Rope binding at George Blair & Co Steel Castings Foundry, Pottery Lane, Newcastle 1943. Right 'Making Munitions' from the 'It All Depends on Me' Ardath tobacco cigarette card set, 1940

The first canteen for the forces run by volunteers of the Women's Voluntary Service opened on platform eight at Newcastle Central Station on 20 November 1939 and in the first six months of its existence over 170,000 members of the forces had been served. In June 1940 a second WVS canteen was opened at the station by Stella Isaacs, Marchioness of Reading, founder and chair of the WVS, who also spoke at a recruiting meeting at King's College, Newcastle, in which she said *'This war is providing women with a wonderful chance to prove their mettle and show to the world that they will not be found wanting.'* Her message was clear, in her concluding remarks at the opening of the canteen she declared *'The dish cloth is mightier than the dress!'* The Central Station WVS canteen on platform eight was open during the daytime and through every night for the majority of the war. Other canteens followed soon after: at the YMCA on Blackett Street, a Salvation Army Servicewomen's Canteen was on St. John Lane, at Salvation Army Hostels, the Old Assembly Rooms on Westgate Road and at the Chronicle Hall on Rosemary Lane.

A unit often overlooked in histories that did so much for troops at home and abroad is the Salvation Army. Among the contingent that proceeded to France was a Newcastle woman, fifty-six year old Mrs Mary Janet Climpson. She had been in France working with the Salvation Army during the First World War and returned shortly after the arrival of the British Expeditionary Force in 1939 with her husband Brigadier Herbert Climpson, who was working as Deputy Director for War Services for the Salvation Army in France. The order had been given to evacuate the headquarters where they were working in Arras and while the pair were making for the channel coast with two co-workers by car in a military convoy on 20 May 1940 they were attacked by an enemy aircraft. Everyone dived out of their vehicles for cover in ditches, but Mrs Climpson was struck by a bomb splinter and killed. She was the first woman to be killed while serving alongside the BEF. Initially buried beside the road where she died, she now rests in Dieppe Canadian War Cemetery, Hautot-Sur-Mer. Mary had relatives living in Newcastle and a special memorial service was held for her at the City Temple when the news of her death reached home.

In Newcastle, and across Britain, women stepped into a host of jobs where men had volunteered or had been called up to serve in the forces. They did almost every job on the railways from shed work and portering to working in gangs on the permanent way and firing locomotives, they took over delivery rounds, became postwomen and worked in more shops and offices than ever before. Newcastle was one of the first police forces to adopt an auxiliary women police corps during the war. The original volunteers were mostly employed on some light police duties, police car and ambulance drivers but the Newcastle Watch Committee decided in favour of the recruitment of women to the Newcastle police force in 1942.

The workforce left at the shipyards after conscription was reduced to young lads, older men and those who had been judged medically unfit for military service. It was the women of the North East who kept the great industries in shipyards and factories running and provided the workforce needed to expand these industries to meet the needs of war production. The shipyards along the Tyne turned out numerous fighting vessels and merchant ships for the war effort. Vickers-Armstrong built munitions, torpedoes and tanks while other companies made a host of equipment and components for ships, military vehicles, aircraft and other military purposes.

In February 1941 it was announced some 2,666 Tyneside women had already left their homes for munitions work in other areas. An appeal for thousands more was placed in the newspapers and a new recruiting office for the Ministry of Labour and National Service opened on Grainger Street. The starting wage for women aged eighteen and over for a 47-hour week varied from 31s to 38s, free fare and payment for travelling were given for the initial journey, the factory work was described as needing 'only a minimum of training' and most women could pick it up within the first fortnight of employment. Actual earnings for those at the new factories averages 40s-45s. When experienced they could earn up to 60s a week and when fully skilled a pay packet of 75s plus overtime awaited them.

Morale was key to keeping up war production; radio programmes like 'Workers Playtime' were often played through factories on loud speakers. Gracie Fields was one of the most popular singers and entertainers of the war years - her pre-war songs such as *'Wish Me Luck As You Wave Me Goodbye'* and *'Sing As We Go'* were revived and soon became anthems for the working people on the home front and those on active service during the war years. Born in Rochdale to a working class family, 'Our Gracie', as she was affectionately known, visited industrial areas all over the country, especially the North, to sing live in concert to boost morale. On 29 July 1941 'Our Gracie' came to Tyneside and performed before one of her largest indoor audiences at one of the great shipyards and in evening she performed again to an audience of more than 4,000.

Initially older women neighbours had been encouraged to act as 'nurseries' for young children so their mothers could go to work, as least as part-time war workers, every hand helped and made a difference. A national poster campaign boldly stated 'Caring for a war workers' children is a National Service', but as demands for war production grew a more organised scheme was required. Newcastle's first wartime day nursery was opened at Ashfield House on Elswick Road by the famous actress Dame Sybil Thorndike on 27 March 1942 and there were plans for another thirty-six more to be opened in the near future in the Northern region.

A lesser-known claim to fame is the role these factories played in the D-Day landings. The contract for waterproofing tanks was placed with a team of experts in Newcastle. There was the call for about 1,000 tons of sheet metal for tanks, which was supplied in quick time from factories in Newcastle, Gateshead, Birtley and Wallsend. They supplied 30,000 feet of suitable chains for flail tanks that made paths through minefields on the beaches, but their greatest claim to fame was that one third of the floating roadway and pier heads of the 'Mulberry Harbour' at Arromanches, which contributed so much to the success of D-Day, were made to a tight deadline and in great secrecy in factories of the Tyne, Tees and Wear.

Women working on the light milling machines at Vickers Armstrong Elswick Works c1940

Men and women working on the lathes in the workshop at Anglo-Scottish Trading Co, toolmakers, New Road, Team Valley Trading Estate 1944.
Below: Women assembling components in the RM Electrics workshop, 1944

LAND GIRLS

Four pals in the Northumberland Women's Land Army, c1942

Plans for the establishment of a Women's Land Army (WLA) to fill the gap in the workforce left by farmworkers called up to military service were laid early in 1938 when organising committees were established in every county. In Northumberland, Countess Grey of Howick was appointed committee chair and they were fortunate to recruit Kathleen Irene Clement of Linnel Dene, Hexham, initially as County Secretary, but as the organisation grew she became County Organiser. The wife of 'Bentley Boys' motor racing engineer and driver Francis 'Frank' Clement, in newspaper reports and correspondence she assumed the formal title of Mrs F C Clement and tirelessly organised the WLA in Northumberland throughout the war.

The first branches of the WLA in Northumberland began training at their 'county agricultural schools' in July 1939. At this stage the training consisted of the women being shown how to drive a tractor and then being given a chance to practise and having the working day on a farm explained to them at an appointed farm for one week. They would then be sent for a further week's training on a private farm in Northumberland. The first farmers training women were Major J G G Rea

Recruitment poster for the Women's Land Army, c1941

the harvest had already been gathered in and a large workforce was not required on the farms at that time but it was fully anticipated that in the spring of 1940, when more men had been called up, many more WLA members would be needed in the county. In the meantime they were only recruiting volunteers for the WLA mobile force, those who were willing to work anywhere in the country.

In January 1940 WLA membership in Northumberland stood at 180 and *The Evening Chronicle* caught up with the progress of local WLA workers by profiling 17-year-old Helen Murdie of Douglas Street, Wallsend:

'A few months ago she was working from 9 till 5 as the junior typist in a Newcastle Quayside lumber office. When war broke out she joined the land army and now her day's work is a vastly different story. Her alarm rings at 6.00am and from 6.30 until black-out time she is hard at it round the farm.

Her first job is to help with the milking. Then there is Frederick, the calf, to feed. Frederick has been 'weakly' but Helen has made him her special care and now he is much better. The hens and pigs come under her care too and between whiles she helps with sorting potatoes and any other odd job that comes her way. In the evenings round the cosy fire in the farm house living room she knits, writes letters or read thrillers as the fancy takes her. And so to bed, her last job is to set the alarm clock again for 6.00 in the morning.'

of Doddington, Wooler and Mr R S Sloan, manager of the Ashington Coal Company's farm at Bothal. In an interview with *The Evening Chronicle* in October 1939, Mrs Clement stated: 'There was a very good response in the county when recruits were asked for and we have 100 on the register, of these thirty are at present being trained or in employment. All farmers who have them speak well of them and are pleased with their progress.'

The problem was that in the early months of the war

When spring of 1940 came, however, there was not a high demand for women working on Northumberland farms because a significant number of farmers maintained a preference for male labour, a view some kept well into the war when they requested work gangs of prisoners of war, often Italians, instead of WLA teams for land work. There were also problems for WLA members. Many of those placed on Northumberland farms from mid-1940, when many men had been called up and the U-Boat menace was claiming thousands of tonnes of merchant shipping, had volunteered when the need for land workers was high and they were sent directly to farms as an extra pair of hands with no training at all. This would be repeated throughout the war and the women would be expected to learn quickly on the job. There were also problems with women being expected to work around the farm house cooking and cleaning as well as their farm work. Many women experienced loneliness, having known town and city life all their lives and suddenly finding themselves stuck in a farm out in the wilds of Northumberland with no transport. Accommodation was also often less than ideal and many women found to their horror that there was nowhere they could take a hot bath; some didn't even have running hot water to clean up after a long day working on the farm.

Many of these issues were experienced by WLA members across the country and schemes were soon introduced to create hostels where the women from different farms could stay, have company with other women and get a shower or hot bath. The first of these in the county were at Haugh Head, Wooler, which was fitted out by the WVS with a volunteer warden, and at Pawston Farmhouse Hostel, near Mindrum, which was run by the Young Women's Christian Association (YWCA), which went on to run many of the WLA hostels in Northumberland. The hostels for WLA members would be staffed by a warden (and an assistant warden at larger establishments), a cook and as some adverts requested 'a good strong girl' who would be employed as a stoker (for the heating and cooking appliances) cum cleaner. Lorries would pick the women up and drop them at the farms in the morning and would come and collect them at the end of the working day. Woe betide the girl who was late!

In January 1941 there were 122 WLA members working on the land in Northumberland but the introduction of conscription for women in 1941 and the increase in numbers of men called up for military service caused bigger and bigger gaps in the home workforce. With the demand for greater agricultural productivity to keep Britain fed, women were needed on the land more than ever and Northumberland WLA was soon enjoying a steady flow of twenty recruits a week by April 1941. Many of them were hairdressers and shop assistants from Newcastle who fancied a taste of the country life. County Organiser Mrs Clements commented in the press: *'Northumberland farmers realise shop assistants and hairdressers make first rate land workers because they are accustomed to being on their feet all day.'* The local women were joined by some of the WLA from Durham; most of them were given placements in the county with others placed in farm or forestry work in Cumberland. By August 1941 numbers were such they were able to supply a contingent of two hundred members of the WLA from Northumberland, Durham and Lancashire to work in Kent and the south of England until spring 1942.

As the demands for silage (animal fodder for the winter) in Northumberland increased a County Silage Officer, Mr D I McLaren, was appointed. A scheme was devised in September 1941 by which WLA members, mainly from Newcastle, were banded into mobile gangs of four to help with the ensilaging of laid corn. Each work gang would have their own caravan to live in, which would be moved with them as they worked from farm to farm and, at least for the time being, addressed some of the accommodation issues. Audrey Lambert of Newcastle, formerly a clerk in an accident claims department and Wynifred Allon of Whitley Bay, a florist, received press coverage for their work travelling in their caravan as the first full-time WLA mobile rat catchers. Their summer caravan, like many of those used by the WLA members at the time was named after a famous hotel, the Ritz-Carlton, but as winter approached Audrey and Wyn were looking forward to staying in a heavier 'winter quarters' caravan they christened 'The Dorchester.' Soon there were a number of rat catching teams of

Members of the Women's Land Army pause for a photo while working at Stocksfield, c1942

three or four WLA women working out of hostels around the county. Bags of 200 rats in a day were known, but in one three-day stint at Pressen Farm near the border, the team from Cornhill hostel bagged over 1,000 rats.

By 1942 160,000 more acres of land, much of it formerly fell and pasture, had been ploughed up and brought to cultivation in Northumberland. The story was being repeated across the country and a national appeal was made for folks to 'lend a hand on the land.' WLA membership was increasing all the time and a new hostel was opening nearly every week; indeed by the spring there were eighteen in the county, fourteen of which were filled to capacity and more were planned. About half the WLA hostels in Northumberland were run by the YWCA. They came in a variety of guises and sizes, from converted railway carriages at Wooler to purpose-built wooden huts and brick buildings - even a few country houses were requisitioned for the purpose. Farmers making use of WLA labour from hostels were asked to provide their own transport wherever possible and gave as much notice to their requirements as they could. This was not always easy when hostels like those at Matfen, Nedderton and Norham did not have telephones. Weekends and certain evenings at the hostel would have entertainments laid on such as whist drives, evening classes in make do and mend, first aid, health, child welfare, current affairs and keep fit. Weekends would occasionally see the hostels lay on parties and dances. There were also local dances where many a wartime romance was kindled. All WLA girls stationed more than twenty miles from home were granted a railway warrant for a visit home every six months.

Members of the public not engaged in war work were encouraged to spend their summer holiday at the special camps set up across the country in agricultural areas.

Women who were too old or too young to join the WLA, or those who could only work part time, could join the Northumberland Guild of Agricultural Workers (NGAW). In May 1942 there were NGAW gangs working in the districts of Alnwick, Seahouses, Rothbury, Hexham, Morpeth and Bedlington. If the farm where they were working at was not on a bus route they were taken to the fields by War Agricultural Executive van. Pay at 10½d an hour was not great and the work, planting potatoes and other root crops, was labour intensive but the women of the NGAW wore their badges of membership with great pride and knew they too were 'doing their bit.'

Tens of girls from the North East had been working in forestry and saw mills for the home-grown timber trade since early in the war but the needs of war production were such that the Ministry of Supply (Home Grown Timber Department) inaugurated The Women's Timber Corps (WTC) as a separate arm of the WLA in 1942. WTC members, nicknamed 'Lumber Jills,' took over just about every job in the industry from skilful measuring, estimating and acquisition to felling and cutting or working with the heavy horses that would haul the cut tree trunk through the forest to the saw mill and the lumber yard. With imports slashed, home-grown wood was essential to the war effort. Wood for military purposes had a huge range of uses from wooden huts and coachwork for lorries and ambulances to ammunition boxes. On the home front wood was needed for important areas of the war effort such as railway sleepers, telephone poles and pit props for coal mines. WTA members were also engaged in charcoal burning from alder buckthorn wood that was indispensable in the manufacture of certain types of explosives. 300 members of the WLA and Timber Corps were invited to attend a party given by the Queen at Buckingham Palace in July 1943. Six members of the Timber Corps who had demonstrated long or good service were selected to go and among them was Miss

The September 1944 edition of The Land Girl, *the monthly magazine of the Women's Land Army.*

Doris Coulson of Newcastle, who had been working in acquisition measuring in Northumberland, Durham and Yorkshire for the three years.

Timber Corps girls had their own billets of various types just like the members of the WLA. Food was not bad at the hostels as girls working on the land or in forests had to eat well. WTC member Stella Carr recorded the menu in rhyme:

On Monday we have sausage fried
On Tuesday egg and spam
On Wednesday we have kippers (dyed)
On Thursday beans and ham
On Friday we have spam and egg
On Saturday first rate salmon
But on my life on Sunday morn,
Real egg and glorious gammon.

That was on a good week. Someone told the cooks that sardines were rich in vitamins and they became a regular feature on the menu. Some of the girls were not too keen on the fish and joked if they could get their hands on that 'someone' they would 'cut him to pit props.'

Pre-service training units for girls entering the women's services had been established in Newcastle but there was still nowhere for those wishing to serve in the WLA. A Northumberland Youth Committee survey revealed the greatest number of girls expressing an interest in joining the Land Army were located in the Byker area so October 1942 saw the formation of a Young Farmers Club at Byker. A site was provided for the new group opposite Welbeck Road School for agricultural experiments and keeping livestock.

Mindful that training would be greatly appreciated by both members of the WLA and farmers, ploughing demonstrations and proficiencies in the likes of dairy and horse husbandry had been staged at agricultural training centre farms such as Cockle Park, Morpeth and Wooler Farm, Wooler since 1941. But there was nothing quite like bringing together larger groups of WLA members, the wider agricultural community and members of the Young Farmers Clubs at competitions held around the county. WLA members would be challenged to find the best with the plough pulled by horse or tractor, fastest chopper out, best hedger or turnip singler. The publicity, good work and a genuine need for the WLA saw membership in Northumberland rise from 373 in December 1941 to its height of 1,386 in December 1943. Recruitment for the WLA was also helped because girls who were volunteering for one of the women's arms of the uniformed services would be told they were not taking any more on at that time and the options left open to them were either munitions work or the WLA.

In 1945 there were 1,250 WLA members working on the land in Northumberland and 865 in County Durham. They had all done their bit, there had been bumper harvests and Britain had been kept fed. The WLA did not end in 1945 but as it was no longer on a war footing many of the girls wanted to return to their old employment or settle down and get married. On Thursday 31 May 1945 many of the girls bade farewell at the county rally of Northumberland WLA held in the grounds of Alnwick Castle. 41 WLA members were presented with their service badges, among them the longest serving 'veteran' of Northumberland WLA, 21-year-old Eleanor Weallans of Lee Farm, Longframlington, who was presented with her 11th badge which represented a total for five and a half years of good service. The WLA was finally disbanded in 1950 and only then did the County Organiser Mrs Clement retire too; recognised with an MBE for her services in 1944, she is believed to be one of only two County Organisers in the country to have served throughout the existence of their county Women's Land Army.

LIFE ON THE HOME FRONT

A family inspect their new Anderson Shelter at Two Ball, Lonnen, Newcastle, March 1939

As Britain teetered on the brink of war in August 1939, people made the best of their leisure time. The summer had been a good one and those who could afford a holiday took it, or at least had a day on the sands at Whitley Bay on the Bank Holiday. The last week in August saw Newcastle and Northumberland life carry on much as it had in holiday time for generations: volunteers gathered some of the beautiful crop of heather at East Shaftoe to sell for the annual appeal for the Newcastle Throat, Nose and Ear Hospital, mothers brought arms full of babies for the Baby Show at Burradon, horse hikers rode their mounts over the moors near Netherwitton, silver bands competed at the Allendale Floral and Horticultural Society Show and the North Eastern Model Aero Club held its members rally on the Town Moor.

On Saturday 2 September 1939, the day before war was declared, the Toon were playing at home against Swansea Town and won 8-2 so a happy atmosphere should have filled the town. Friends met for a special afternoon tea, accompanied by the pleasant sound of Gary Bland and the tea room band, at the terrace tea room at Fenwick's, where freshly buttered white and brown bread, cream scones and raspberry jam with Devonshire cream accompanied by China or Indian tea, could be enjoyed for 1s 3d. The cinemas in Newcastle were showing a host of popular films. *No! No! Nanette* was ending its run at The Royal and Albert Modley, 'The Great Little Yorkshire Comedian', was appearing at the Empire while the Haymarket cinema was showing Gary Cooper in *Beau Geste*, The Essoldo had Mickey Rooney, Lew Stone and Cecelia Parker in *The Hardys Ride High* and the Queen's and Pavilion were promoting Will Hay in *Ask A Policeman* showing the following week. Somewhat poignantly, the Olympia on Northumberland Road was showing *The 39 Steps* starring Robert Donat. Attendance was down at all these events and entertainments because thousands of children had been evacuated, male and female Territorials had received warning orders for mobilization or were already mobilized and many men had been called up. With numbers down and the war looming, some events such as the Shotley Bridge Agricultural Society show, Wolsingham Show, the annual demonstration of Houghton le Spring Divisional Labour Party, the Newcastle CWS and the Scotswood Amateur Swimming Galas were cancelled altogether and the White City (Newcastle) Greyhound stadium announced there would be no more racing until further notice. The Roker Illuminations that had been erected for a massive £8,000 were, in the light of black-out restrictions, 'postponed.'

The war emergency situation was evident in the newspapers too. Currys Newcastle store advertised a portable radio, ideal for air raid shelters as 'your link in an emergency'; there were columns explaining how to protect against bombs in an air raid by digging a shelter trench or making a refuge room and how to limit bomb blast damage by applying 'stout paper or rubberised tape' to windows. An urgent appeal was made for 8,000 blood donors to come forward on Tyneside.

Newcastle residents who had neglected to collect their gas masks after a warning to do so were going in ever increasing numbers to pick them up from their local ARP depots. Similarly, hundreds of people who took no notice of earlier advice not to stockpile or 'hoard' food started a rush on certain shops. Provision dealers sold out of tinned foodstuffs and in many cases could not provide disappointed customers with a definite date for future deliveries. City shops certainly did a roaring trade, selling thousands of yards of blackout cloth for use as window blinds and door curtains as well as torch batteries and gas proof jars and containers.

All large stores in Newcastle and Gateshead had undertaken extensive plans for the safeguarding of their staff and customers which included training the staff in first aid, fire extinguishing and controlling crowds, in addition to reinforcing basements and other shelters. Some decided to follow the example of certain London firms and close their premises for a few days if war should be declared. At another store a *Weekly Chronicle* reporter was informed:

'In the event of an air raid the customers will have to obey the instructions of the staff who will guide them to places of safety. We have wardens for every section and sub-section of our store in addition to fire stations and a small but efficient fire-fighting service of our own. We are doing everything we can to ensure the safety of customers and to avoid panic.'

The manager of another unnamed store was less accommodating: *'Immediately an air raid warning is given the doors of the premises will be closed and the staff will take up the positions allotted to them. We will look after the customers who are in the shop but cannot allow people in the streets to take shelter.'*

War was declared at 11.00am on Sunday 3 September 1939. Sunday services at cathedrals, churches and chapels all had congregations many times their usual size and the news of the state of war between Britain and Germany was relayed to congregations by the priests in their pulpits across Newcastle and Tyneside.

The Lord Mayor, Alderman W R Wallace, toured the city after the declaration was made and was able to report that it was a *'wonderful example of organisation and the cool, collected spirit ... the city is bearing up splendidly.'* The news was not greeted as it had been in 1914, when there was cheering, streamers and dancing in the street. The lessons of that war had been painfully learned.

As in the Great War, however, thousands came to Newcastle to join up. Hundreds of young men left their homes outside the city in the early hours, some from as far away as Berwick, to arrive at the Combined Recruiting Centre at the YMCA Boys' Club on Maple Terrace, off Scotswood Road, long before its doors were open. When he did eventually greet the volunteers, Major Frank Ward, Northumberland Zone Recruiting Officer, saw a queue of over 150 men but as the centre was only staffed to take 60 a day, they simply could not cope with the rush. A steady stream of students applying for commissions also enrolled at the No.7 Reception Unit in the College Union Buildings at King's College. At the National Service Recruiting Centre on Northumberland Street. Mr G B Neal, who was handling enrolment forms, stated 450 enrolled on 4 September and a further 500 before noon on 5 September.

In the immediate aftermath of the declaration of war all theatres, cinemas and places of entertainment were closed by government order. If enemy bombers did suddenly spring an attack the authorities wanted to avoid large concentrations of people at all costs. When the closure order was imposed there was no indication of a possible re-opening date. Fortunately they were permitted to open again from 15 September and managers took pains to announce in newspapers that everything possible had been done to ensure the safety of patrons, all precautions had been taken to observe black-outs, all staff had been drilled in emergency duties and were ready to act as wardens and fire fighters at a moment's notice. In Newcastle the initial scheme was that they would open from 11.00am to 9.30pm to enable patrons to catch public transport home. It was a land of black-outs, gas masks carried everywhere, uncertainty, patriotism and stoicism.

Morale in wartime is so important and many dignitaries came to Tyneside to see the mines, factories and shipyards and their workers during the war. First among them was Winston Churchill, when he was First Lord of the Admiralty, on a two-day visit in December 1939. Wherever the man went he was greeted with cheers and a large crowd gathered on the platform at Central Station to wave and cheer as he departed. As Churchill made his way to the train a workman shouted: *'You'll beat Old Nasty yet!'*, which Churchill greeted with a resolute smile and a wave of his hat. Churchill returned in late July 1940, this time as Prime Minister. As Britain faced the very real danger of invasion after the fall of France, Churchill toured the country to inspect coastal fortifications and defence works. On his visit to Tyneside he also made a point of visiting a shipyard where he was given an enthusiastic reception by workers and their wives. Churchill also made a surprise visit on 7 November 1941 to visit bomb-damaged areas and industrial concerns on Tyneside.

The King and Queen visited shipyards and armament factories on 18 June 1941 and the Princess Royal took great interest in the operations of the headquarters of the Northumberland and Durham War Needs Fund headquarters on 17 July 1941. The King and Queen returned in April 1943 visiting Byker and Heaton.

Prime Minister Winston Churchill on one of his visits to the North East during the Second World War

A great way to bring a country together is to get it working together in a common cause. Within months of the outbreak of war in far more of a 'we are all in it together' exercise than any real need for scrap iron, the first appeals were made for surplus ironwork. Private garden railings, railings around public parks, Victorian features, statues and even trophy guns and tanks from the Great War that had been given to towns and cities after the end of the war were taken away for scrap 'for the war effort.' Newcastle Corporation made a good start by taking up disused tram lines in Barrack Road, Shields Road and Stanhope Street. Approximately 1,000 tons of high-grade material were obtained in this way and delivered to the Ministry of Supply. Donations by local firms saw thousands of tons collected in Newcastle and 477 sets of garden railings were taken away for scrap metal. Scrap Metal Week in July 1940 encouraged people to bring their scrap to 'dumps' set up to the east or west of Pilgrim Street.

As more drives were introduced for collections for the likes of rags, metal, rubber, paper, bones or scraps for pig food, many areas were very grateful to the WVS or Women's Institute for providing a Salvage Officer to

Removing garden railings to obtain scrap iron 'for the war effort' at Oakhurst Terrace, Benton, 1940

oversee the collections. By the end of November 1940, 850 pig bins were in use in Newcastle, collecting around 29 tons of scraps every week.

One of the most unusual appeals came as make-up became harder to obtain. An appeal went out to those who had taken part in amateur dramatics and to theatrical stores for grease paint or make-up of any description that could supply any of the sixty concert parties operating in the north east in which some 1,600 volunteer artistes were taking part. By the end of 1940 the concert parties had presented over 100 shows a week, travelled 150,000 miles and entertained over half a million service personnel – all for expenses only - which cost the grand sum of £974 2s 11d, all paid for by the war needs fund.

After the initial closures shortly after the outbreak of war, most of the Newcastle places of entertainment soon got back on their feet. The Theatre Royal staged plays, ballet opera and musical comedy, there were news theatres on Pilgrim Street and at The Tatler on Northumberland Street. The Newcastle Repertory Company regularly performed at the Playhouse, Jesmond and the People's Theatre, Rye Hill and Little Theatre, Fern Avenue, also hosted occasional amateur performances.

The Empire, Newgate Street and Palace, Percy Street offered music hall entertainment. There were a host of cinemas to choose from: The Essoldo, Westgate Road; The Grainger, Grainger Street; Haymarket, Barras Bridge; New Westgate, Westgate Road; Odeon, Pilgrim Street; Pavilion, Westgate Road, Queen's Hall

Applying to change their retailers ration books at the Food Control Office, Newcastle, January 1941

Northumberland Street and Stoll, Westgate Road. All Newcastle cinemas were closed on Sundays but film shows for the services were staged on Sunday evenings at the YMCA and light concerts were held at the City Hall.

Dances were always popular and were held every day except Saturdays and Sundays at the Oxford Galleries on New Bridge Street. Bi-weekly dances were held on Wednesdays and Saturdays at the Old Assembly Rooms on Westgate Road and there were frequently dances for the various war charities. Dancing lessons were provided at the Central Dance Studios on Blackett Street and the Newbegin Dance Studios at St Andrew's Buildings (West).

Concerns over what would happen if people were 'bombed out' of their homes were well thought out and a number of rest centres were established in the city. Newcastle inaugurated a communal feeding scheme that would form the basis of the distribution of free meals after air raids. The first three communal feeding centres in the city opened at Victoria Jubilee School, Royal Jubilee School and Elswick Road School on 8 October 1940. Those who were not 'bombed out' could also purchase well-balanced cooked meals to take home at extremely cheap prices. The menu on the first day consisted of:

Soup..1d
Soup with Dumplings.................1½d
Meat dish......................................3d
Pudding...2d

Schools heartily took on the 'Dig for Victory' campaign too as seen here with the girls from Whickham View School in 1943

Despite food rationing being introduced in January 1940, there were still acute shortages at times. In late January 1941 housewives arrived to do their daily shopping at the Grainger Market to find the majority of butchers' stalls closed down. Of other meats such as turkey, chicken, goose or rabbit, only rabbit was within the means of most people and on one occasion a queue of 80 women extended from the rabbit meat stall when the stallholder had only 38 rabbits left to sell. *The Evening Chronicle* reported *'The women seemed to take the battle for rations in good spirit but now and again there was bumping and boring and a verbal battle as to who had been first in the queue.'*

In wartime, before most people were aware of the dangers of smoking, many people took up the habit to steady their nerves. Imagine the horror in February 1941 when shortages occurred and over fifty city centre tobacconists displayed notices stating they had no supplies. The newspapers reported Newcastle was suffering a 'cigarette famine.' Many blamed the situation on the recent air raids and even though it was claimed in the House of Commons that there was no shortage of supplies in the North East, it took a while for stocks to be replenished in Newcastle shops. Such situations always give rise to entrepreneurs and more than one cinema manager got his cleaners to collect the stubs from ash trays in separate bags and set up small teams to earn a bit of extra money picking the stubbed cigarettes apart to remove what tobacco was left and using rolling machines and cigarette papers to create new packs of cigarettes, which they re-sold under mysterious brand names in the cinema entrance kiosks. Although often in short supply or subject to accusations of being watered down, beer was never rationed.

By 1943 so many young men and women had been

One of three new buses ready to join the Newcastle Corporation Transport fleet and the staff that built it at Northern Coachbuilders, June 1939. Below: A Wartime knitting pattern for soldier's comforts.

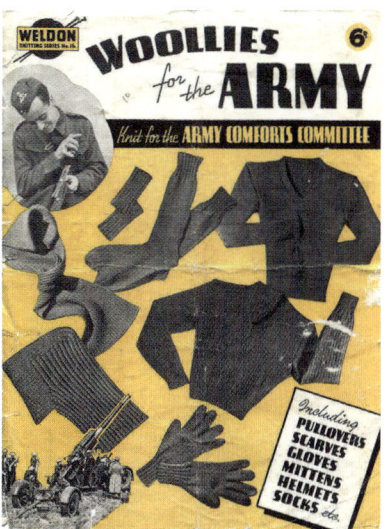

called for military service that some shops did experience staffing difficulties and closed for an hour at lunch times, opened for fewer hours and closed all day on Sundays. By that time the purchase of any new clothing, boots, shoes, foods, soaps, chocolate or sweets required ration coupons. Hats were not rationed, neither were shaving soap, cosmetics, toothpaste or food eaten in restaurants or cafes.

To help produce more food everyone was encouraged to turn their garden into a vegetable patch or take on an allotment. Large areas of land in public parks was also put to cultivation. In March 1943, Newcastle held its 'Dig for Victory' Week at the Northumberland Road Baths Hall, which included a special exhibition to encourage people to grow the sort of food that would see them through the winter. At the opening a message from Mr R S Hudson, Minister of Agriculture, stated

Knitting party for comforts for servicemen at Park View House, Heaton November 1939

that Newcastle's Dig for Victory Week should be *'the starting point for an all-out effort to produce vegetables on every available plot of land in the district.'*

Newcastle, just like every other British city, helped other cities when they were bombed by sending supplies of blankets and clothes and helping raise funds to provide food and comforts for those who had lost everything. Newcastle Corporation even loaned fourteen blue double decker buses (the bus livery was blue in wartime) to London Passenger Transport in October 1940 after the capital's fleet had been severely damaged during the blitz. On the instruction of the Minister of Transport, when the buses returned to Newcastle in 1941 a plate bearing the simple inscription 'London 1940-41' was inserted in each vehicle to mark their 'blitz service.'

In 1940 Newcastle led the country per head of population in its contributions to the British Red Cross Society and Order of St John Penny-a-Week Fund to help fund medical supplies and parcels for prisoners of war.

To avoid duplication of effort the Northumberland and Durham War Needs Fund was formed in 1940 by the amalgamation of a number of war charities that had been established early on in the war, specifically the *Journal* and *North Mail* and *Evening Chronicle* War Fund, The Lord Mayor of Newcastle's War Needs Fund the *Shields Gazette* Merchant Seamen's Fund, the Mayoress of Jarrow's Comforts Fund and the Whitley Bay and District Air Raid Victims' Fund. The first flag day collection for the amalgamated groups in Newcastle raised the magnificent sum of £1,111 6s 11d. On New Year's Day 1941 the Northumberland and Durham War Needs Fund was able to announce they had received £43,000 in donations to help the war needy in the North East, sending knitted socks, balaclavas, gloves

Certificate given to children for making donations to the 1940 Empire Day fund that helped the Overseas League provide comforts for troops.

and scarves to local lads in uniform on land and sea and parcels of comforts to prisoners of war. By the end of the war the fund had raised £250,967.

This was no mean feat and owed a great deal to the women of the two counties who knitted the comforts at a rate of thousands a month. The Women's Institutes, with Mrs Baker Cresswell at their head in Northumberland and Mrs Lloyd Pease in County Durham, were stalwarts in their support for fundraising and knitting of the comforts. At the War Fund's Comforts Depot in Lovaine Row, Newcastle, voluntary workers under the leadership of Mrs R. Mould Graham and Miss Alison Nicholson as secretary worked long days at sorting and packing. By the end of 1940 over 80,000 garments had passed through their hands. But this had only been made possible thanks to the generosity of workers in the North East, who donated coppers from their wages that ensured a regular income for the fund. Even smaller funds dedicated to supporting men from a particular area or battalion produced impressive amounts of comforts; a prime example was the Ladies Committee of the Tyneside Scottish who, by December 1944, had been responsible for 8,260 knitted items and 500 parcels sent for prisoners of war and a further 400 comforts knitted for their men in the forces.

Every year there would be a range of smaller events and fundraisers for war charities and one really high profile drive over a week of special events, parades, concerts and displays staged around the city to motivate local firms and individuals to raise and lend money for the war effort by purchasing National Savings Stamps, Certificates and War Bonds that would be paid back with a little interest after the war. One of the earliest, staged during the Battle of Britain, was The Spitfire Fund, inaugurated on 20 August 1940, to provide a Spitfire or Hurricane that would bear the name Newcastle upon Tyne. Streets and districts clubbed together to raise money, a variety of fund raising events were staged, there was even a sweepstake of the number of enemy planes to be brought down run by the local ARP depot. The fund raised over £3,000.

September 1940 saw Tyneside's War Weapons Week. Among the highlights were the O'Gorman brothers, surrounded by the glamour girls from the Newcastle Empire, who sold savings stamps in Eldon Square and the engine of a Junkers that had been shot down was put on display at the Essoldo cinema. Two Czech girls, Miss Sigmund and Miss Olapso, keen to do their bit for the country that provided them with a home, spent hours collecting money for the funds at the Tatler café. An elderly lady arrived at a cinema kiosk to buy War Bonds with her savings, which amounted to £43 – in threepenny bits. The Tyneside War Weapons Week raised and incredible £3,000,000.

In February 1941 Newcastle and Gosforth stepped up to the mark again for Warship Week, with an original target of £1,750,000 the aim was to adopt HMS *Newcastle* but with over £3,750,000 raised there was even enough money for a sister ship. Among the fund raisers were Misses Lena and Flossie Simpson who held a bring and buy sale at their house on Lily Crescent, Jesmond, and eight-year-old Charlie Ratcliffe of Chillingham Road raised 25 shillings by organising a raffle.

In September 1942 the news of Adam Wakenshaw's VC reached Newcastle. He was the first Newcastle resident to receive the Victoria Cross during the war. A native of Newcastle, the youngest of thirteen children, he had worked in the pits since he was fourteen. In one of the first interviews after the announcement of his award was made public his mother said: *'I'm not surprised a lad of mine should get the VC for I was a Moran before marriage and the Morans were fighting Irishmen one and all.'* Remembered as a loving father and man who would do anything for anyone, he left a wife Dorothy and two

Advert for the Newcastle and Gosforth Warship Week, February 1941

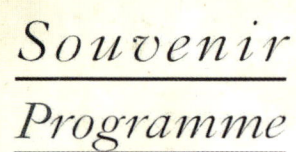

Boxing Tournament to raise funds for Mrs Winston Churchill's Aid to Russia Fund and Northumberland and Durham Ward Needs Fund, 1942

children, Tommy (7) and Lily (3) (his eldest son had been run over and killed by a rolley when he was playing near his home in 1941). It was reported *'of material things he had virtually nothing and his home is in a poor district of Newcastle.'* The Wakenshaw VC Shilling Fund was organised and thousands of pounds were raised through voluntary donations for the care of his family.

The last big War Savings drive was Salute the Soldier week in April 1944. Highlights included parades and

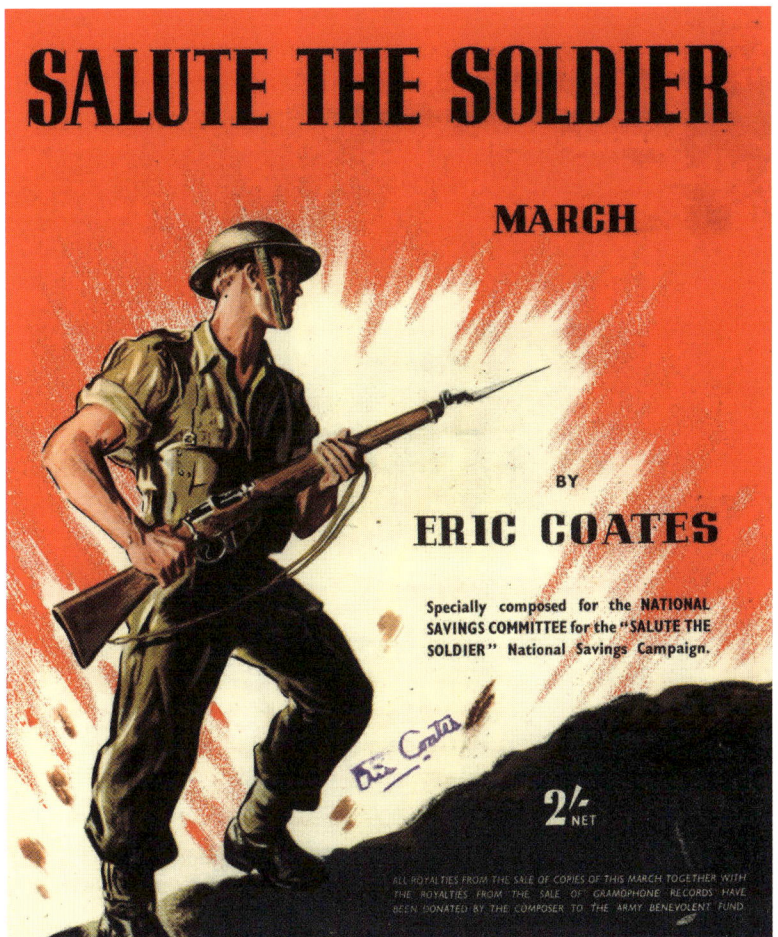

march pasts by a host of uniformed organisations including Home Guard, Army Cadets, Air Training Corps, the band of the Tyne North Sector Home Guard and the pipe band of 9th Battalion, Northumberland Home Guard. Massed bands played marches and Captain CEB Howes narrated the achievements and gallantry at a special tribute to 50th Division and a physical drill display by National Fire Service women at Gosforth. One of the most impressive spectacles was the closing concert at the City Hall with the Royal Marines salute to the soldier with bands from the RN School of Music and the RM concert dance orchestra. The progress of the funds

The last big drive for War Savings were the Salute the Soldiers weeks of 1944

Below: Miners with pit ponies and coal tubs were part of the Newcastle Victory Parade, 1946.
Left: Miners and 'Bevin Boys' at the parade

raised was recorded by a 'Tommy Atkins' soldier at Grey's Monument whose arm gradually rose to a perfect salute. Newcastle and Gosforth came up trumps again raising £3,356,867.

Miners did their bit too!

In the early years of the Second World War the government allowed experienced coal miners to be called up for military service. Miners were also allowed to transfer to higher paid work in other reserved occupations, the hope being that the gaps in the mining industry would be taken by the unemployed. By mid-1943 over 36,000 coal miners had left the industry and the unemployed seemed more keen to take just about any other work, even volunteering to join the forces, than work down a pit. That said, it should not be forgotten that many pre-war miners remained down the pits and worked long and hard shifts to help keep up production and lads as young as fourteen were attending the training pit at Ashington from 1940 to enable them to start working down the mines of Northumberland.

The problem was there still were not enough miners to keep producing the supplies of coal to meet wartime demands. By October 1943 it was claimed Britain was down to just three weeks of coal supplies in reserve. To remedy the situation Ernest Bevin, the Minister for Labour and National Service, devised a scheme whereby a ballot took place to allocate half the intakes of conscripted men to serve down the mines rather than in the armed forces.

A total of 48,000 'Bevin Boys' were thus conscripted, half by the ballot with no other option and the remainder came by choice in preference to serving in the armed forces. Between 1943 and 1945 one in ten conscripted soldiers were sent to work down the mines. The first batch of 600 Bevin Boys began training for work in the pits on 18 January 1944. Their training lasted six weeks, four off site and two on. The Bevin Boy programme was finally wound up in 1948.

VICTORY!

One of the Newcastle street parties to celebrate VE Day, May 1945

On 8 May 1945, the war in Europe came to an end with the unconditional surrender of Nazi Germany and Britain celebrated VE Day with street parties and huge crowds in every market place. Even the poorest streets in Newcastle and Tyneside managed to club together and pool ration coupons to do something to celebrate but as many pictures show it was a day mostly for the children. A more formal parade of both military and civilian forces followed by a Thanksgiving Service was held at St James' Park on 13 May. The war had only just finished and was only celebrated at home by those already on leave; it would be weeks and months before many others were demobilized, released from military service and came home in their snappy 'demob suits.'

On 26 August 1945 a Victory march was staged in Newcastle. An estimated 100,000 people lined the route as the two-mile long parade marched by. Meanwhile the men in the Far East, often known as 'The Forgotten Army' (and they felt this when they heard of such

Military and civilian forces join together in front of a capacity crowd for the Victory in Europe Thanksgiving Service at St James' Park on 13 May.

events back home) were fighting an all too real war in the jungles of India and Burma while others endured captivity in Japanese hands. Eventually the Japanese surrendered and VJ Day was celebrated on 2 September 1945. It would take months for the men and women of all services to get home from the furthest-flung corners of the war, but they were brought together for final Victory parades in 1946 when the majority were home again. Contingents from all regiments, including the Royal Northumberland Fusiliers, joined the Victory Parade in London. Newcastle held its Victory parade on 8 June and staged a Victory Tattoo at the City Hall on consecutive nights 8-10 June 1946.

The Newcastle Victory Parade assembled on Barrack Road and marched up Gallowgate, Blackett Street and

The magazine for troops in the Far East was called Victory although it was years between its initial publication and VJ Day in 1945

A smart turnout from the RAF contingent on the Newcastle Upon Tyne Victory Parade, June 1946

past Eldon Square where the Lord Mayor took the salute with representatives of HM Forces. The parade then marched on through the city centre to Northumberland Street. It was headed by detachments from the mounted motorcyclists of the Corps of Military Police, a Troop of Medium Guns of the Royal Artillery, a Light AA Troop and the Royal Artillery and an armoured car Troop from the Royal Armoured Corps, followed by the Royal Armoured Corps Band and detachments representing The Royal Navy, The WRNS, The Royal Northumberland Fusiliers, ATS, RAF, WAAF, The Merchant Navy, The Tyne (North Sector) Home Guard Military Band, a parade of the demobilised services, the Old Coldstreamers Association, The 'Old Contemptibles' Association, The Band and Standards of the British Legion, Newcastle City Police Band, members of the St John Ambulance, British Red Cross Society, a symbolic mother riding in the Lord Mayor's coach followed by 'The Queue of Housewives' in salute to the mothers and housewives of Britain, Women's Voluntary Services and Women's Land Army followed by a wonderful array of youth groups, a historical cavalcade and a tribute to service and industry including miners complete with pit ponies and tubs, munitions workers, National Fire Service, Post Office, Canteen Services, 'Clippies' and Drivers of Newcastle City Transport and Firewatchers.

It was a great parade and was all the more impressive because of the pains that were taken to represent all the local lads and lasses who 'did their bit' at home and abroad during the Second World War. The war touched everyone who lived through the years 1939-1945 in Newcastle and Tyneside; some of them suffered life-changing injuries to body or mind or both. For many the new challenge was getting to know their families again after years of separation and trying to rebuild their lives in peacetime.

The Finale of the Victory Tattoo that was staged at City Hall 8-10 June 1946. Left: Souvenir programme for the Newcastle Upon Tyne Victory Celebrations, June 1946. Right: Booklet issued to men and women leaving the services

APPENDICES

APPENDIX 1.

THE EVACUATION OF SCHOOLCHILDREN FROM NEWCASTLE 1 SEPTEMBER 1939

The majority of children were evacuated by school from Newcastle. This list shows the schools in alphabetical order along with their detraining stations. Some schools have two entries because children from the same school were evacuated to different locations. Please note: not all the children would have remained in these towns, a number would have been given homes in the outlying villages and farms around the area.

Akhurst Preparatory...........................Penrith, Cumberland
Atkinson Road...............................Egremont, Cumberland
Atkinson Road, Junior Technical......................Workington, Cumberland
Bentinck......................................Windermere, Westmorland
Benwell, South..................................Lazonby, Cumberland
Bolam Street Special …....................Silecroft, Cumberland
Canning Street..................................Aspatria, Cumberland
Canning Street......................................Wigton, Cumberland
Central Newcastle High School......Keswick, Cumberland
Chillingham Road.......................Belford. Northumberland
ChillinghamRoad..............Tweedmouth, Northumberland
Church High School (Girls Secondary).......................Alnwick, Northumberland
Convent de la Sagesse (R.C. Secondary Girls)..............Berwick, Northumberland
Convent of Sacred Heart.................Kendal, Westmorland
Cowgate......................................Hexham, Northumberland
Cowgate**.................................Wooler, Northumberland
Cragside Junior and Infants........................Morpeth, Northumberland
Cruddas Park..........................Cockermouth, Cumberland
Cruddas Park...........................Keswick, Cumberland
Cruddas Park...........................Wigton, Cumberland
Dame Allan's ....Wigton, Cumberland
Delaval................................Haltwhistle, Northumberland
Denton Road...............................Brampton, Westmorland
Denton Road...........................Kirkbride, Cumberland
Denton Road..........................Silloth, Cumberland
Elswick Road Girls
....Wallington Hall, Northumberland
Fenham R. C. …................................Kendal, Westmorland
Gateshead (Boys)....................................Drigg, Cumberland
Gateshead(Girls) ....Silecroft, Cumberland
Heaton Junior Technical....................Millom, Cumberland
Heaton Park Road...............Bellingham, Northumberland
Heaton, Secondary Boys............Whitehaven, Cumberland
Jesmond, West..........................Rothbury, Northumberland
Lower Condercum Special....................Drigg, Cumberland
Municipal College of Commerce
....Brampton, Westmorland
Newcastle Preparatory............Rothbury, Northumberland
Newcastle Preparatory
.... Eslington Hall, Whittingham, Northumberland
North Heaton...................Tweedmouth, Northumberland
North View..................................Alnwick, Northumberland
North View..................................Wooler, Northumberland
Northern Counties Inst. for the Deaf *
................................North Seaton Camp, Northumberland
Pendower Commercial and Technical
....Workington, Cumberland
Pendower Elementary
....Haydon Bridge, Northumberland
Pendower Elementary......................Dalston, Westmorland

Pendower Open Air * ....North Seaton Camp, Northumberland
Royal Grammar................................Penrith, Cumberland
Royal Jubilee Junior and Infants ....Morpeth, Northumberland
Spital Tongues Junior and Infants..............................Alnwick, Northumberland
Rye Hill R.C. …..................................Aspatria, Cumberland
Rye Hill R.C..Maryport, Cumberland
St. Aloysius R. C. …...............Cockermouth, Cumberland
St. Aloysius R. C..............................Wigton, Cumberland
St. Aloysius R. C.........................Workington, Cumberland
St. Andrew's ....Wigton, Cumberland
St. Bede's R.C. ....Kendal, Westmorland
St. Cuthbert's Gram...............Cockermouth, Cumberland
St. Dominic's R.C. …................Hexham, Northumberland
St. John's C. E. …............................Seascale, Cumberland
St. Joseph's R.C. ....Egremont, Cumberland
St. Lawrence's R.C...................Morpeth, Northumberland
St. Mary's R. C. ....Windermere, Westmorland
St. Mary's R. C.................................Maryport, Cumberland
St. Mary's R.C..................................Aspatria, Cumberland
St. Michael's R.C. Infants...........Whitehaven, Cumberland
St. Teresa's R.C............................Amble, Northumberland
Todd's Nook ....Kendal, Westmorland
Victoria Jubilee.....................Alnmouth, Northumberland
Walker, East..............................Hexham, Northumberland
Walker, West..............................Hexham, Northumberland
Walker Gate.................................Brampton, Westmorland
Walker Gate …........................Cockermouth, Cumberland
Westmorland Road ....Cockermouth, Cumberland
Westmorland Road ....Maryport, Cumberland
Westmorland Road …........................Millom, Cumberland
Wingrove …..Kendal, Westmorland

* Transported by Education Committee's bus
** Transported by United bus

APPENDIX 2

ORGANISATION OF THE FIRST AID, AMBULANCE AND EMERGENCY HOSPITAL SERVICES

Originally published as an Appendix to the Report of the MOH, by Dr J. A. Charles, MD, FRCP dated January 1940.

1) The organisation of the First Aid, Hospital and Ambulance Services, which has been called into being as a result of the national emergency is briefly as follows:
    (1) First Aid Parties
    (2) First Aid Posts
    (3) Ambulance Services
    (4) Emergency Hospitals
        (a) Casualty Receiving Hospitals
        (b) Base Hospitals

The precise role which is being played by each of the above and their detailed organisation will be described in order in the subsequent paragraphs. A short account of the methods of communication and co-operation with and between the various units of the scheme and the other constituent elements of the ARP organisation is included.

2 FIRST AID PARTIES

In theory the First Aid parties should consist of 5, or at least 4 men, one of whom is also a driver, as the Parties are intended to be mobile. For this purpose each party should be provided with a car.

At the outbreak of war the strength of the First Aid Party personnel was not more than 150 men, and it was necessary to undertake the most energetic recruitment in order to raise the numbers to the minimum required for the service to be operative at all.

As a result of these efforts the effective establishment is now -

        Whole-time men............386
        Part-time men................109

The establishment provided 2 reliefs for 97 First Aid Parties, each of 2 whole-time men, with a number of part-time volunteers in reserve for times of activity. The First Aid Party thus consists of 2 men, i.e. the minimum necessary to carry a stretcher.

Considerable difficulty has been experienced in obtaining a suitable type of man for whole-time employment with First Aid Parties. A large number of volunteers have come forward, but after interview, medical examination, and preliminary training, only a proportion can be regarded as likely to make effective whole-time personnel.

With regard to part-time personnel, only a relatively limited number of men have volunteered and in view of the fact that there will always be an uncertainty with regard to the availability of part-time personnel it is proposed to regard the part-time establishment as a second line, rather than to depend upon its members for immediate service after an air-raid.

It is thus necessary to have available a minimum number of whole-time personnel, and for this purpose a proposed establishment of 388 has been submitted to the Regional Commissioner.

With regard to the transport of the First Aid Parties, it was decided early after the outbreak of war that in order to obtain the maximum degree of efficiency from the small number of First Aid personnel available, the Parties should be linked as closely as possible with the ambulances by using the latter as their means of movement from place to place. (The cars allowed for the use of the First Aid Parties have not been employed in consequence of the introduction of this arrangement). Each First Aid party – Ambulance Unit consists of (a) the vehicle, (b) its driver, and (c) 2 trained First Aid men. The 97 First Aid parties and the 97 ambulances associated with them constitute an integral part of the 75 Point Scheme, upon which the passive defence of the City is based. The 75 Point Scheme ensures that every part of the City is within reach of a Depot or Sub-Depot at which are stationed representative sections of some or all of the services – First Aid, Ambulance, Auxiliary Fire Service, Rescue and Demolition, and Decontamination. The distribution of the First Aid Parties and their associated ambulances is set out below:-

2 cars and First Aid Parties at each of the 15 Key Depots = 30 cars and 30 First Aid Parties

1 car and 1 First Aid Party with each of the remaining 60 Sub-Depots = 60 cars and 60 First Aid Parties

7 cars with the Central Reserve of 7 First Aid Parties stationed at the Central Control = 7 cars and 7 First Aid Parties

Total = 97 cars and 97 First Aid Parties

3 FIRST AID POSTS

The appropriate number of First Aid Posts for a city with the population and area of Newcastle upon Tyne is 15. During the early months of 1938 an extended search for premises suitable to be used as First Aid Posts was made and over 150 buildings were inspected and measured. Only nine were found which were able to provide the necessary requirements, and these buildings, after adaptation and protection, constitute the City's First Aid Posts. Owing to the relatively small number of Posts available, i.e., nine instead of 15, and the large size of the premises used, authority was given for correspondingly enlarged establishments of personnel. In addition sanction was obtained for the attachment of two medical practitioners to each Post instead of the usual establishment of one.

At the commencement of the war the selected buildings were not in a high state of readiness structurally owing to the delays which had transpired in obtaining the approval of the Ministry of Health for the necessary adaptations. But the work of conversion was rapidly completed and the essential protective works were also carried out. Equipment had never been a difficulty, as the Health Committee had obtained large stocks during the 1938 Crisis, and these had subsequently been augmented by Government issues.

The location of the 9 Posts is as follows:-

No. of Post

1. Central School, Pendower................................Tel: 34732
2. Elswick Hall, Elswick Park..............................Tel: 34733
3. Dame Allan's School, Bolbec Road.................Tel:34162
4A. Elementary School, Snow Street.................Tel: 35014
4B. Newcastle Dispensary, 115 New Bridge Street
....Tel: 27946
5. Royal Grammar School, Eskdale Terrace
....Tel: Jes. 1639
6. Public Baths, Chillingham Road.....................Tel: 56316
7. Elementary School, Raby Street....................Tel: 56326
8. Public Baths, Wharrier Street......................... Tel: 63394

The staff allotted to each Post is as follows:-

a) Medical officer, 2 (Part-Time)
b) Whole-time Nursing and First Aid Personnel:-
    Trained Nurse – 1
    Male First Aid Personnel – 4
    Female First Aid Personnel and Nursing
    Auxiliaries – 21
Total whole-time personnel = 26 (4 male, 22 female)
c) Part-time First Aid Personnel:-
    Male First Aid Personnel – 4
    Female First Aid Personnel - 30

Hours of Duty
a) The posts are open continuously day and night.
b) Whole-time personnel work 8-hour shifts and have one completely free day in seven.
c) Part-time personnel attend as and when it may be convenient for them to do so.

Functions
The main functions of a First Aid Post is to admit minor casualties and to give to the individuals concerned such treatment as may be necessary. After they have received attention, such cases are sent home, with instructions to return to the Post for further treatment, or to attend their family practitioner. They may also be despatched to hospital for x-ray examination, special treatment, etc.

Serious casualties occurring in the vicinity of a First Aid Post are admitted to the Post, and subsequently transferred to the Casualty Receiving Hospitals. Other serious casualties are collected by the First Aid Party and Ambulance System and brought to the Post (but not admitted) so that the Medical Officer in charge of the Post can confirm the diagnosis and give any immediate essential treatment or advice as to the care of the patients undergoing transportation. The patients are then despatched to the Casualty Receiving Hospitals.

4 AMBULANCE SERVICES

The approved establishment of ambulances and cars for sitting cases allowed for this City is at present 145 ambulances and 97 cars. Prior to September 1939 the Ambulance Officer had arranged for the earmarking of a considerable proportion of the vehicles required to function as ambulances and the smaller cars required for sitting casualties. Five motor engineering firms had placed their premises at the disposal of the City for use as Maintenance Depots. The stretcher-carrying fitments and other equipment for the ambulances were stored at these depots and were issued to the vehicles on mobilisation. The largest number of vehicles mobilised at any one time was 121 ambulances and 55 sitting cars, and these numbers have been reduced by the release of certain vehicles until the actual strength now is 118 ambulances and 48 sitting cars. Very shortly after mobilisation it became evident that the hire and maintenance of these vehicles, many of which were in a decrepit condition, was likely to involve an exceedingly large expenditure. The details in respect of the ambulances mobilised during the month of September were as follows:

Hire	£1,905
Repairs and Maintenance	£484
Petrol and Oil	£260
Total	£2,649

In view of these facts, representations were made to the Ministry of Health on the 21st September suggesting that the vehicles requisitioned for ambulance duties should be replaced by large private motor cars which could be purchased and converted into light ambulances at a relatively low cost. This recommendation was agreed to by Ministry and Health Circular 1893 issued on the 20th October. As soon as the requisite authority had been obtained steps were taken to acquire, either by gift or purchase, a sufficiency of ambulances to replace the majority of the old van type of ambulance. So far, 35 light ambulances have been obtained by the method indicated, and an equivalent number of requisitioned vehicles released.

The Home Office and the Ministry of Health have recently suggested that the number of ambulances constantly on duty should be reduced to one-third of the total establishment, and that the balance of the original establishment might be obtained from the auxiliary establishment consisting of vans in ordinary employment which would report at Ambulance Stations as and when required. Representations have been made to the effect that these suggestions are impracticable in so far as this City is concerned. It is agreed, however, that some reduction can be effected in the authorised establishment of ambulances and cars for sitting cases, and the following establishment has been put forward:-

Ambulances........................96
Cars for sitting cases.........56

5 EMERGENCY HOSPITALS

In order to provide adequate arrangements for the treatment of casualties, emergency hospitals are provided both within and outside the areas they are intended to serve. Those located in the area constitute Casualty Receiving Hospitals, those outside are regarded as the Base Hospitals. Usually the number of beds in Base Hospitals far exceeds the number in the institutions reserved for the reception of casualties.

In the Newcastle area, however, owing to the fact that the bulk of hospital accommodation for Northumberland and Tyneside is concentrated in the City, and the consequent absence of suitable hospitals in the adjacent areas, it was found necessary, temporarily at any rate, to reverse the normal arrangement. At the present time the majority of the emergency hospital beds are situated within the city, and in fact the normal establishment of beds has been considerably augmented by the erection of additional beds both in the existing wards and in other accommodation within the hospitals. The Base Hospitals outside, although each possessing a nucleus of bed accommodation, are still in progress of development and construction.

The policy of the Ministry of Health, in so far as base Hospitals are concerned, has been to take an existing institution and build in association with it large hutments, comprising hospital wards, kitchens, operating theatres, etc. Such hutted hospitals are at present in course of erection at Shotley Bridge, Stannington and Hexham. When these Base Hospitals are complete, their total compliment of beds will exceed the accommodation in the casualty receiving institutions in Newcastle.

The emergency hospitals for the City have been organised in two groups – municipal and voluntary respectively. The constitution of these groups and the beds which will be ultimately available at the individual hospitals are set out in the following tables. (It should be understood that in addition to the hospitals included in the latter, there are a number of other institutions, e.g., the City Mental Hospital, Gosforth, at which beds have also been provided.)

It will be noted that at the institutions owned by the City Council, e.g., Newcastle General Hospital, Elswick Grange, and Shotley Bridge Colony, no fewer than 2,000 casualty beds will be available.

Despite the fact that large numbers of beds are reserved specifically for the reception of casualties, the hospitals in Newcastle are still able to treat every patient who requires their services. The work of augmenting the accommodation in the hospitals has entailed the provision of large stocks of beds, blankets, drugs, dressings, surgical instruments and x-ray apparatus. In the main this has been done by the Ministry of Health, though in certain cases valuable apparatus owned by the hospitals in the City has been transferred on loan to the Base Hospitals outside.

MUNICIPAL GROUP

Newcastle General Hospital
Function in time of war: Civilian Sick and Casualty Reception
Beds available for casualty purposes: 512
Beds available for civilian sick and other purposes: 502

Elswick Grange (a)
Function in time of war: Civilian Sick and Casualty Reception
Beds available for casualty purposes: 621
Beds available for civilian sick and other purposes: 415

Shotley Bridge M.D. Colony (b)
Function in time of war: Base Hospital
Beds available for casualty purposes: 884
Beds available for civilian sick and other purposes: 250

Hexham P.A. Institution (a)
Function in time of war: Base Hospital
Beds available for casualty purposes: 500
Beds available for civilian sick and other purposes: 87

VOLUNTARY HOSPITALS

Royal Victoria Infirmary
Function in time of war: Civilian Sick and Casualty Reception
Beds available for casualty purposes: 662
Beds available for civilian sick and other purposes: 438
Fleming Memorial Hospital
Function in time of war: Civilian Sick and Casualty Reception

Beds available for casualty purposes: 92
Beds available for civilian sick and other purposes: 30

Sanderson Hospital School
Function in time of war: Casualty Reception
Beds available for casualty purposes: 195
Beds available for civilian sick and other purposes: ---

Stannington Sanatorium (c)
Function in time of war: Base Hospital
Beds available for casualty purposes: 578
Beds available for civilian sick and other purposes: 310

Stannington Mental Hospital (d)
Function in time of war: Base Hospital
Beds available for casualty purposes: 500
Beds available for civilian sick and other purposes: 700

Note: (a) = aged and infirm; (b) = mental defectives; (c) = tuberculosis; (d) = mental cases

Nursing Staff

The greatly increased accommodation in the hospitals has necessitated considerable additions to the nursing personnel. These have been provided through the channel of the Local Emergency Committee for the Nursing Profession, which has been able to utilise the resources of the St. John Ambulance Brigade and the British Red Cross Society. It has also undertaken the organisation of a large number of volunteers who have elected to be trained under municipal auspices. This nursing personnel constitutes the local section of the Civil Nursing Reserve. At the present moment 232 of them are employed at the various hospitals in the two groups on a whole-time basis, while 330 others give part-time service or are standing by ready to serve when required. In addition, 700 are in course of training, and will be available for hospital duty in the immediate future.

6 COMMUNICATIONS, PROCEDURE FOR DISPOSAL OF CASUALTIES, LINES OF EVACUATION, ETC.

COMMUNICATIONS

The First Aid parties and Ambulance Services are intimately linked with the 75 Points Scheme. Under this scheme a certain degree of autonomous action is permitted to the Directors or Sub-Directors of the Depots or Sub-Depots. Every Depot or Sub-Depot is in communication with the Sub-Control Centres and Central Control by means of direct telephone lines, First Aid Posts and hospitals, though not in direct line telephonic communication with the ARP system can be reached through the ordinary telephone service or by runner.

DISPOSAL OF CASUALTIES

The procedure laid down for the collection and disposal of casualties is briefly as follows:-
On the occurrence of any incident requiring First Aid services, a motor ambulance, carrying a First Aid Party in addition to its driver, proceeds from the Depot or Sub-Depot, picks up the casualty and transports it to the nearest First Aid Post. The casualty is not necessarily admitted to the First Aid Post, but is seen by the Medical Officer of the Post, who determines whether the wound or injury is so severe as to necessitate immediate transportation to hospital, or alternatively is of a less degree of severity which would allow of its treatment at the First Aid Post. After transferring the patient to hospital or leaving him at the First Aid Post the ambulance returns to its Depot or Sub-Depot.

LINES OF EVACUATION

From all points within the area of B Division Sub-Control Centre (which is the same as "B" Police Division), and from the First Aid Posts Nos. 1, 2, 3, and 4A, casualties are referred in the first instance to the Newcastle General Hospital. From the remainder of the City, i.e. from the areas of A and C Divisions Sub-Control Centres, and from the First Aid Posts Nos. 4B, 5, 6, 7 and 8 they are sent to the Royal Victoria Infirmary. These arrangements would obviously be modified if and when one or other of the hospitals is filled to capacity.

APPENDIX 3

NORTHUMBERLAND HOME GUARD

Northumberland District Duty Sectors

Alnwick Sub District

Morpeth Sector
3rd, 10th, 14th, 17th Battalions, Northumberland Home Guard

North Northumberland Sector
1st, 2nd, 16th Battalions, Northumberland Home Guard

Tyne Sub District
4th, 13th Battalions, Northumberland Home Guard

Seaton Sector
5th, 6th, 15th, 18th Battalions, Northumberland Home Guard

Tyne North Sector
7th, 8th, 9th, 11th, 12th Battalions, Northumberland Home Guard

Tyne South Sector
8th, 10th, 21st, 25th Battalions, Durham Home Guard

Durham Sub-District
18th, 20th Battalions, Durham Home Guard

Consett Sector
1st, 2nd, 3rd, 4th, 5th, 6th, 23rd Battalions, Durham Home Guard

Houghton le Spring Sector
11th, 12th, 13th, 14th, 22nd, 26th Battalions, Durham Home Guard

Weardale Sector
15th, 16th, 17th Battalions, Durham Home Guard

Sunderland Garrison
7th, 9th, 24th Battalions, Durham Home Guard

8th Anti-Aircraft Regiment Home Guard

101 County of Durham Home Guard
Anti-Aircraft Rocket Battery, South Shields

103 County of Durham Home Guard
Anti-Aircraft Rocket Battery, Sunderland

101 Northumberland Home Guard
Anti-Aircraft Rocket Battery, Whitley Bay

71st Battalion, Durham Home Guard
Heavy Anti-Aircraft Rocket Battery, Gateshead

71st Battalion, Northumberland Home Guard
Heavy Anti-Aircraft Rocket Battery, Newcastle

Northumberland Home Guard Battalion Headquarters and Commanding Officers as at 'Stand Down' 1944

1st Battalion (Berwick) Lieutenant Colonel Sir Alfred Goodson Bt.

2nd Battalion (Alnwick) Lieutenant Colonel H R Milvain

3rd Battalion (Morpeth) Lieutenant Colonel G L Rutherford

4th Battalion (Hexham) Lieutenant Colonel J R Robb OBE

5th Battalion (Gosforth) Lieutenant Colonel R S Barrett

6th Battalion (Blyth) Lieutenant Colonel N O Parry

7th Battalion (Tynemouth) Lieutenant Colonel S Holmes

8th Battalion (Wallsend) Lieutenant Colonel A Walker

9th Battalion (Central Newcastle) Lieutenant Colonel B. Donaldson

10th Battalion (Otterburn) Lieutenant Colonel A H Ridley

11th Battalion (West Newcastle) Lieutenant Colonel E K Clifford

12th Battalion (East Newcastle) Lieutenant Colonel J Macdonald OBE MC

13th Battalion (19th GPO) (Newcastle) Lieutenant Colonel F Johnston

14th Battalion (Bedlington) Lieutenant Colonel A Laird MC

15th Battalion (Forest Hall) Lieutenant Colonel H W Brass

16th Battalion (Amble) Lieutenant Colonel C Y McNay

17th Battalion (Ashington) Lieutenant Colonel B Cruddas DSO

18th Battalion (Seaton Delaval) Lieutenant Colonel J A Metcalf

Northumberland Home Guard Transport Column (Newcastle)
Lieutenant Colonel E Jowett

APPENDIX 4

CIVILIAN CASUALTIES COMMEMORATED BY THE COMMONWEALTH WAR GRAVES COMMISSION AT NEWCASTLE UPON TYNE COUNTY BOROUGH CEMETERIES

Reproduced by kind permission of the Commonwealth War Graves Commission

ACASTER, Robert William, age 53, died 30 Dec 1941, Air Raid Warden. Husband of May E. Acaster, of Duren, Eastfield Road, Benton. Injured 29 December 1941, at Station Approach, Benton; died at Royal Victoria Infirmary.

AIKEN, William, age 43, died 25 April 1941, 3 Stannington Road. Died at Cheltenham Terrace.

AIREY, Ethel Mary, age 23, died 25 April 1941, 10 Guildford Place, Heaton. Daughter of Francis and Ethel Mary Park; wife of Pte. William C. Airey, The Durham Light Infantry. Died at 10 Guildford Place.

ALEXANDER, Alfred, age 17, died 1 Sept 1941, Son of Harry and Ellen Alexander, of 9 Gladstone Street. Died at Camden Street.

ALEXANDER, Sara Ann, age 28, died 1 Sept 1941, 25 Camden Street. Wife of Pte. Harry Alexander, Royal Army Medical Corps. Died at Camden Street.

ALLEN, Margaret, age 67, died 1 May 1942, 12 Coley Hill Terrace, North Wallbottle. Daughter of the late Thomas and Elizabeth Cowan; wife of Albert James Allen. Injured at 12 Coley Hill Terrace; died same day at General Hospital.

ALLINSON, Charles Henry, age 39, died 1 Sept 1941, Firewatcher; of 196 Grace Street, Byker. Son of William and Sidella Allinson, of 7 Blount Street, Byker; husband of Esther Allinson. Died at 181 Grace Street.

ANGUS, Amy, age 17, died 25 Apr 1941, 13 Guildford Place, Heaton. Daughter of the late Thomas M. and Martha Angus. Died at 13 Guildford Place.

ANGUS, Edna Jane, age 28, died 25 Apr 1941, 13 Guildford Place, Heaton. Daughter of Hannah Angus; wife of Robert Nixon Angus. Died at 13 Guildford Place.

ANGUS, Hannah, age 49, died 25 Apr 1941, 13 Guildford Place, Heaton. Daughter of Isabella and of the late John T. Harrison; widow of Thomas M. Angus. Died at 13 Guildford Place.

ANGUS, Ian, age 3, died 25 Apr 1941, 13 Guildford Place, Heaton. Son of Robert Nixon Angus and Edna Jane Angus. Died at 13 Guildford Place.

ANGUS, Maureen, age 15, died 25 Apr 1941, 13 Guildford Place, Heaton. Daughter of the late Thomas M. and Martha Angus. Died at 13 Guildford Place.

ANGUS, Robert Nixon, age 29, died 25 Apr 1941, A.F.S.; of 13 Guildford Place, Heaton. Son of the late Thomas M. and Martha Angus; husband of Edna Jane Angus. Died at 13 Guildford Place.

BALMER, Mary Elizabeth, age 17, died 25 Apr 1941, Daughter of William and Esther Balmer, of 8 Ronald Drive, Denton Burn. Died at 12 Guildford Place.

BARWICK, Elizabeth Mould, age 55, died 29 Dec 1941, 45 Matthew Bank, Jesmond. Daughter of Matthew and Lizzie Ann Winship, of 16 Londonderry Street, New Silksworth, Sunderland; widow of the Revd. Joseph Barwick. Died at Matthew Bank.

BEATTIE, William Lumsden, age 61, died 28 Jan 1941, Son of the late Robert and Sarah Beattie, of Front Street, Hobson Colliery; husband of Mary Ann Beattie, of 91 Middle Street, Walker-on-Tyne. Injured 27 January 1941, at Walker Naval Yard; died at Royal Victoria Infirmary.

BLAND, Joseph, age 39, died 22 May 1943, 55 Viceroy Street. Husband of Mary Bland. Injured 6 May 1943, at Seaham Harbour; died at General Hospital.

BLENKINSOP, William, age 38, died 25 Apr 1941, 6 Tosson Terrace, Heaton. Died at 12 Guildford Place, Heaton.

BOUSFIELD, Lily, age 58, died 29 Jul 1940, 31 Forsyth Road, West Jesmond. Daughter of Adam Bousfield. Died at 31 Forsyth Road.

BRADSHAW, Thomas, age 19, died 2 Sept 1941, Son of Mr. and Mrs. Patrick Bradshaw, of 145 Walker Road. Injured at St. Peter's; died same day at Royal Victoria Infirmary.

BURNEY, Annie, age 30, died 1 Sept 1941, 121 Union Road, Byker. Daughter of Annie Burney, and of the late Henry Burney. Died at 121 Union Road.

BURNS, Mary Murray, age 24, died 1 Sept 1941, 123 Union Road, Byker. Daughter of Anie Corby, of 41 Eastern Way, Blakelaw Estate, and of the late William Corby; wife of William Burns. Died at 123 Union Road.

BURNS, Maureen Murray, age 13 months, died 1 Sept 1941, 123 Union Road, Byker. Daughter of William Burns, and of Mary Murray Burns. Died at 123 Union Road.

CAMPANY, Robert George, age 31, died 1 Sept 1941, husband of Ethel Campany, of 1 Turner Street. Died at Stoddart Street.

CARRIGAN, Isabella, age 65, died 1 Sept 1941, 127 Union Road, Byker. Wife of James Carrigan. Died at 127 Union Road.

CHARLTON, Alexander Anderson, age 63, died 30 May 1943, of 72 Stainton Street, South Shields. Son of the late Peter and Isabella Charlton. Injured 24 May 1943, at Stainton Street; died at General Hospital.

CHIVERS, Ronald, age 11, died 30 Dec 1943, Injured in Bedlington; died at the Royal Victoria Infirmary, Newcastle-upon-Tyne. Killed by exploding rifle grenade in Bedlington, Northumberland.

CLARK, Margaret, age 32, died 1 Sept 1941, 57 City Road. Daughter of Patrick and Maria Malice, of 59 City Road; wife of Pte. William Clark, Pioneer Corps. Died at 57 City Road.

CLARK, Maureen Veronica, age 2, 1 Sept 1941, 57 City Road. Daughter of Pte. William Clark, Pioneer Corps, and of Margaret Clark. Died at 57 City Road.

COULSON, Anne Blackburn, age 4, died 1 Sept 1941, daughter of James Coulson, of 15 Turner Street, and of Isabella Coulson. Died at Turner Street.

COULSON, Isabella, age 43, died 1 Sept 1941, wife of James Coulson, of 15 Turner Street. Died at Turner Street.

COULSON, James, age 17, died 1 Sept 1941, son of James Coulson, of 15 Turner Street, and of Isabella Coulson. Died at Turner Street.

CUNNINGHAM, John Patrick, age 79, died 1 Sept 1941, 119 Union Road, Byker. Husband of Catherine Cunningham. Died at 119 Union Road.

CUNNINGHAM, Laura Elizabeth, age 12, died 1 Sept 1941, 119 Union Road, Byker. Daughter of Catherine Cunningham, and of John Patrick Cunningham. Died at 119 Union Road.

CURRY, George, age 41, died 27 Nov 1943, Firewatcher. Husband of A. J. Curry, of 82 Haig Crescent, West Benwell. Died at City Road.

DAGLISH, Robert, age 59, died 29 Dec 1941, Firewatcher; of 78 Dalton Street, Byker. Died at Dalton Street.

DAVIDSON, William Edward, age 64, died 12 May 1941, 4 Farquhar Street, Jesmond. Husband of Eleanor Weddell Davidson. Died at 4 Farquhar Street.

DAWSON, Robert Furness, age 56, died 1 Sept 1941, 57A City Road. Husband of Sarah Isobel Dawson. Died at 57A City Road.

DAWSON, Sarah Isobel, age 52, died 1 Sept 1941, 57A City Road. Wife of Robert Furness Dawson. Died at 57A City Road.

DAWSON, William Wilson, age 13, died 1 Sept 1941, 57A City Road. Son of Robert Furness Dawson, and Sarah Isobel Dawson. Died at 57A City Road.

DOBSON, Arthur Ernest, age 42, died 25 Apr 1941, husband of Annie Dobson, of 35 Auckland Avenue, Darlington, Durham. Died at Heaton Assembly Rooms.

DOCKERTY, James, age 78, died 1 Sep 1941, 22 Glasshouse Road. Died at 7 St. Michael's Road

DODGSON, Albert Greenfield, age 56, died 18 Sept 1941, Firewatcher; of 10 Delacour Road, Blaydon-on-Tyne, Durham. Husband of Emily Dodgson. Injured 1 September 1941, at 10 Delacour Road; died at General Hospital.

ELLIOTT, Evelina Elizabeth, age 50, died 1 Sept 1940, 5 Jenifer Grove, High Heaton. Wife of Tom Elliott. Died at 5 Jenifer Grove.

ERSKINE, John McKnight, age 20, died 25 Apr 1941, 12 Guildford Place, Heaton. Died at 12 Guildford Place.

FALCUS, James, age 45, died 25 Apr 1941, 12 Cheltenham Terrace. Died at Cheltenham Terrace.

FARRELL, Ethel, age 37 died 16 Apr 1942, wife of Joseph Michael Farrell, of 10 Simpson Terrace, Shieldfield. Injured 15 April 1942, at Shieldfield; died at Royal Victoria Infirmary.

FRASER, Ethel, age 45, died 30 Dec 1941, 31 Keyes Gardens, Jesmond. Wife of Handley Howard Fraser. injured 29 December 1941, at 31 Keyes Gardens; died at Royal Victoria Infirmary.

FULLER, Albert George, age 37, died 25 Apr 1941, son of Albert George and Ellen Fuller, of 23 Staindrop Crescent, Darlington, Durham. Died at 8 Guildford Place.

GARDNER, Gordon, William Thomas, age 25, died 25 Apr 1941, Firewatcher. Son of the Revd. F. C. Gardner and E. Gardner, of The Manse, Falstone, Hexham. Died at 13 Guildford Place.

GARROD, Eveline, age 49, died 1 May 1942, of Cragside View, Benton Park Road. Wife of Frederick Charles Garrod. Died at Cragside View.

GARROD, Frederick Charles, age 19, died 1 May 1942, Merchant Navy; of Cragside View, Benton Park Road. Son of Frederick Charles Garrod, and of Eveline Garrod. Died at Cragside View.

GIBSON, Frank, age 32, died 4 Sept 1941, Fireman, N.F.S. Son of Taylor and Flora Gibson, of 13 Edwins Avenue South, Forest Hall; husband of Maggie Keen Gibson, of 58 Balmoral Terrace, Heaton. Injured 1 September 1941, at Forth Goods Station; died at Royal Victoria Infirmary.

GLASS, Elizabeth, age 53, died 25 Apr 1941, 12 Guildford Place, Heaton. Widow of Robert Glass. Died at 12 Guildford Place.

GREAVES, Nora Rheuhema, age 25, died 1 May 1942, of Newquay, Benton Park Road. Daughter of Capt. and Mrs. E. H. E. Burdon, of 4 Alderwood Crescent, Walkerville; wife of Albert Greaves. Injured at Benton Park Road; died same day at Royal Victoria Infirmary.

GREEN, Matthew George, age 52, died 20 Sept 1944, Leading Fireman, N.F.S. Husband of Florence Grace Green, of 117 Holystone Crescent. Died at Walkergate Hospital.

GRIFFITHS, George, age 62, died 3 Sept 1941, 27A Yorkshire Street. Died at Royal Victoria Infirmary.

HAGON, Edith Rosina, age 8, died 25 Apr 1941, 11 Guildford Place, Heaton. Daughter of John Thomas Hagon. Died at 11 Guildford Place.

HAGON, Joan Thompson, age 30, died 25 Apr 1941, 11 Guildford Place, Heaton. Wife of John Thomas Hagon. Died at 11 Guildford Place.

HAGON, Joyce, age 16, died 25 Apr 1941, 11 Guildford Place, Heaton. Daughter of John Thomas Hagon. Died at 11 Guildford Place.

HAGON, Raymond, age 7, died 25 Apr 1941, 11 Guildford Place, Heaton. Son of John Thomas Hagon. Died at 11 Guildford Place.

HARRISON, Isabella, age 77, 25 Apr 1941, of 13 Guildford Place, Heaton. Daughter of the late John and Hannah Turnbull; widow of John Thomas Harrison. Died at 13 Guildford Place.

HARRISON, Isabella, age 47, died 1 Sept 1941, 44 Athol Street, St. Peter's. Widow of William Harrison. Died at 44 Athol Street.

HARRISON, James Ford, age 12, died 1 Sept 1941, 44 Athol Street, St. Peter's. Son of Isabella and of the late William Harrison. Died at 44 Athol Street.

HEADS, Percy Scott, age 65, died 21 Oct 1941, 4 Ashwood Crescent. Died at 1014 Shields Road.

HOGGETT, William Henry, age 39, died 26 Apr 1941, Cheltenham Terrace. Died at Cheltenham Terrace.

JAMIESON, William, age 53, died 26 Aug 1944, Husband of Florence A. Jamieson, of 13 Fernlea Road, Balham, London. Injured 27 July 1944, at 15 Culverden Road, Balham; died at Newcastle-upon-Tyne General Hospital.

JENKINSON, Thomas, age 39, died 24 Oct 1941, A.R.P. Demolition Worker. Son of Margaret Jane Jenkinson, of 2 Prince Consort Road, Hebburn-on-Tyne, Co. Durham, and of the late Thomas Jenkinson; husband of Mary Jenkinson, of 89 Cuthbert Street, Hebburn-on-Tyne. Injured 21 October 1941, at Demolition Post, Glen Street, Hebburn-on-Tyne; died at General Hospital.

JOBLING, Edward, age 66, died 8 Dec 1941, 51 Tarset Street, Battlefield. Husband of Henrietta Jobling. Died at 51 Tarset Street.

JOBLING, Henrietta, age 60, died 8 Dec 1941, 51 Tarset Street, Battlefield. Wife of Edward Jobling. Died at 51 Tarset Street.

JOHNSON, George Robert, age 61, died 31 May 1943, Air Raid Warden. Husband of Emma Johnson, of 21 North Crescent, Murton, Co. Durham. Injured 24 May 1943, at Dalton-le-Dale A.R.P. Post; died at General Hospital.

JORDAN, Caroline Margaret, age 61, died 29 July 1940, of 245 Farndale Road. Wife of John Edward Jordan. Died at 245 Farndale Road.

KAY, George, age 9, died 1 Sept 1941, 8 Rock Terrace, Shieldfield. Son of Tpr. Christopher Kay, Royal Tank Regiment, and of Jemima Kay. Died at 8 Rock Terrace

KAY, Jemima, age 32, died 1 Sept 1941, 8 Rock Terrace, Shieldfield. Wife of Tpr. Christopher Kay, Royal Tank Regiment. Died at 8 Rock Terrace.

KELLY, John, age 28, died 2 Jul 1940, Son of John and Catherine Kelly, of 64 Midway, Walker. Died at Spillers, The Close.

KENDAL, Agnes, age 44, died 1 Sept 1941, 33 Sarah Street, Shieldfield. Wife of Henry Kendal. Died at 33 Sarah Street.

KENDAL, Henry, age 12, died 1 Sept 1941, 33 Sarah Street, Shieldfield. Son of Henry Kendal, and of Agnes Kendal. Died at 33 Sarah Street.

KENDAL, Margaret, age 16, died 1 Sept 1941, 33 Sarah Street, Shieldfield. Daughter of Henry Kendal, and of Agnes Kendal. Died at 33 Sarah Street.

KENDAL, Mary, age 18, died 1 Sept 1941, 33 Sarah Street, Shieldfield. Daughter of Henry Kendal, and of Agnes Kendal. Died at 33 Sarah Street.

KERR, David Taunch, age 20, died 29 Jul 1940, Son of Elizabeth Kerr, of 11 Lynmouth Place, High Heaton. Injured 28 July 1940, at High Heaton; died at Royal Victoria Infirmary.

KING, Kate, age 57, died 4 Oct 1941, Daughter of Samuel and Jane Atkinson, of 17A New Queen Street, Scarborough, Yorkshire; wife of Ernest King, of 69 Maple Drive, Northstead, Scarborough. Injured 18 March 1941, at Scarborough; died at General Hospital.

LAMB, Derek, age 6, died 2 Sept 1941, 17 Turner Street. Son of Gnr. Richard Lamb, R.A., and Harriet Lamb. Injured 1 September 1941, at 17 Turner Street; died at General Hospital.

LAMB, Sylvia, age 6 months, died 1 Sept 1941, 17 Turner Street. Daughter of Gnr. Richard Lamb, R.A., and Harriet Lamb. Injured at 17 Turner Street; died same day at General Hospital.

LAWSON, Mary Eleanor, age 58, died 12 May 1941, S.R.N.; of 23 Sturdie Gardens, Jesmond. Daughter of the late John James and Isabella Ann Lawson. Injured at 23 Sturdie Gardens; died same day at Royal Victoria Infirmary.

MACKAY, Mary Isabella, age 44, died 29 Jul 1940, Wife of W. G. Mackay, of 99 Weldon Crescent, High Heaton. Died at School House, Newton Road.

MACLEOD, Winifred, age 39, died 12 Mar 1943, 28 The Oval, Walker Road. Wife of Duncan Alan Macleod. Died at 28 The Oval.

MAIR, George, age 68, died 2 Sept 1941, Firewatcher. Husband of Mary Mair, of 83 Walker Road. Died at Quayside

MARCUS, Cissie, age 26, died 29 Dec 1941, daughter of Barnet Marcus, of 107 Park Avenue, Gosforth. Died at Matthew Bank.

MARSDEN, Alexander, age 36, died 1 Sept 1941, husband of Dorothy Marsden, of 31 Palm Avenue, Fenham. Died at St. Mary's Place

MOEN, Odvar Marius, age 22, died 2 Sept 1941, Norwegian Subject; of 63 Osborne Road. Injured at Jesmond Road; died same day at Royal Victoria Infirmary.

MOFFIT, Mary Jane, age 62, died 25 Apr 1942, daughter of the late Mr. J. Moffit. Died at 9 Guildford Place, Heaton.

MORALEE, Louise, age 55, died 4 Oct 1941, wife of James Moralee, of 58 Chichester Road, South Shields, Co. Durham. Injured 30 September 1941, at Chichester Road; died at General Hospital.

MUNCASTER, Matthew, age 70, died 1 Sept 1941, 1256 Walker Road. Died at the Batey Metallic Factory, St. Lawrence Road

MUNRO, Archibald Taylor, age 29, died 25 Apr 1941, 12 Guildford Place, Heaton. Died at 12 Guildford Place.

MURRAY, Victor, died 6 Oct 1940, Superintendent, City of Newcastle Police Fire Brigade. Husband of M. L. Murray, of 50 Redheugh Road, Gateshead, Co. Durham. Died at Newcastle.

NELSON, Mary, age 36, died 10 Jun 1943, wife of Thomas Nelson, of 35 The Avenue. Injured 16 May 1943, at Sunderland; died at General Hospital.

O'DONNELL, Mary, age 67, died 1 Sept 1941, 67 Clarence Street, Shieldfield. Widow of Cornelius O'Donnell. Died at 67 Clarence Street.

PARK, Ethel Mary, age 60, died 25 Apr 1941, 10 Guildford Place, Heaton. Wife of Francis Park. Died at 10 Guildford Place.

PARK, Francis, age 58, died 25 Apr 1941, 10 Guildford Place, Heaton. Husband of Ethel Mary Park. Died at 10 Guildford Place.

PARK, Mavis, age 31, died 25 Apr 1941, 10 Guildford Place, Heaton. Daughter of Francis and Ethel Mary Park. Died at 10 Guildford Place.

PARMLEY, Mary Anderson, age 54, died 1 May 1942, W.V.S.; of Turra, Benton Park Road. Wife of John Henry Parmley. Died at Turra, Benton Park Road.

PARMLEY, Olive Eleanor, age 61, died 1 May 1942, wife of William Alexander Parmley, of 1 Leslie Crescent, Gosforth. Died at Benton Park Road.

PEEL, Mary Ellen, age 57, died 16 Nov 1941, 258 Shipley Street, Byker. Widow of William Stainthorpe Peel. Injured 6 May 1941, at 258 Shipley Street; died at 272 Shipley Street.

PEEL, William, Stainhope, age 65, died 6 May 1941, 258 Shipley Street, Byker. Husband of Mary Ellen Peel. Died at 258 Shipley Street.

PRUDHOE, John Lee, age 50, died 1 Jan 1942, son of Jane Lee Prudhoe, of 38 Walker Road; husband of Ellen Lee Prudhoe, of 221 Simondside Terrace, Heaton. Injured 29 December 1941, at Dalton Street; died at Royal Victoria Infirmary.

REED, Alice Jane, age 61, died 30 April 1941, 14 Guildford Place, Heaton. Wife of Joseph Dixon Reed. Died at 15 Guildford Place.

REED, Joseph Dixon, age 68, died 30 Apr 1941, 14 Guildford Place, Heaton. Husband of Alice Jane Reed. Died at 15 Guildford Place.

REED, Joseph Lancelot, age 2 months, died 30 Apr 1941, son of Lancelot and Emily Reed, of 2 Railway Cottages, Leadgate, Co. Durham. Died at 9 Guildford Place, Heaton.

RIDLEY, Thomas Chilton, age 29, died 12 Oct 1942, 31 Eastfield Avenue, Monkseaton. Son of Thomas Chilton Ridley, and Elizabeth Ann Ridley, of 8 Springfield, North Shields; husband of Catherine Ridley. Injured 11 October 1942, at Eastfield Avenue; died at General Hospital.

ROBSON, Eliza Margaret, age 70, died 25 Apr 1941, 4 Cheltenham Terrace, Heaton. Wife of William Robson. Died at 4 Cheltenham Terrace.

ROBSON, Ella Mildred, age 43, died 25 Apr 1941, 4 Cheltenham Terrace, Heaton. Daughter of William and Eliza Margaret Robson. Died at 4 Cheltenham Terrace.

ROBSON, Evelyn, age 38, died 25 Apr 1941, 4 Cheltenham Terrace, Heaton. Daughter of William and Eliza Margaret Robson. Died at 4 Cheltenham Terrace.

ROBSON, James Kenneth, age 19, died 25 Apr 1941, at 8 Guildford Place, Heaton.

ROBSON, Mary Jane, age 61, died 6 May 1941, 233 Shipley Street, Byker. Wife of Robert Robson. Died at 233 Shipley Street.

ROBSON, William, age 72, died 25 Apr 1941, 4 Cheltenham Terrace, Heaton. Husband of Eliza Margaret Robson. Died at 4 Cheltenham Terrace.

ROWAN, John, age 60, died 26 Nov 1943, A.R.P. Ambulance Driver. Husband of Florence Rowan, of 568 Denton Road, Denton Burn. Died at 568 Denton Road, as the result of an illness contracted whilst on duty in June 1942.

RUTHERFORD, Thomas, age 18, died 7 May 1942, of Temperance Street. Son of Mr. J. Rutherford. Died at Royal Victoria Infirmary.

SCOTT, Anne, age 25, died 1 Sept 1941, wife of John Robert Scott. Died at 59A City Road.

SCOTT, John Robert, age 27, died 1 Sept 1941, husband of Anne Scott. Died at 59A City Road.

SCOTT, William, age 45, died 1 Sept 1941, son of Harry Scott, of 165 Somerset Street, Hull, Yorkshire; husband of Cicely Scott, of 60 Tosson Terrace, Heaton. Died at 44 Athol Street.

SHANKS, Gilbert, age 31, died 1 Sept 1941, Patrol Officer, N.F.S. Husband of Annie Shanks, of 30 Turbinia Gardens. Died at Northumberland Road.

SHAW, Thomas, age 48, died 25 Apr 1941, Air Raid Warden; of 14 Cheltenham Terrace, Heaton. Died at Cheltenham Terrace.

SHAW, William Atkinson, age 40, died 25 Apr 1941, Air Raid Warden; of 14 Cheltenham Terrace, Heaton. Died at Cheltenham Terrace.

SHILLINGLAW, Robert age 50, died 1 Sept 1941, Home Guard; of 29 Sarah Street, Shieldfield. Husband of Dora Mary Shillinglaw. Died at 29 Sarah Street.

SHORT, George, age 55, died 1 Sept 1941, Firewatcher; of 60 Athol Street, St. Peter S. Died at 44 Athol Street.

SLOAN, John, age 33, died 1 Sept 1941, 20 St. Oswald's Avenue. Died at St. Mary's Place.

SLOANE, Gladys Mildred, age 41, died 29 December 1941, 43 Matthew Bank, Jesmond. Daughter of Mr. and Mrs. Patterson, of Brandling Village; wife of William Sloane. Died at 43 Matthew Bank.

SMITH, Henrietta, age 30, died 8 Dec 1941, wife of Sto. James Smith, R.N. Died at 57 Tarset Street.

SMITH, James, age 3, died 8 Dec 1941, son of Sto. James Smith, R.N., and of Henrietta Smith. Died at 57 Tarset Street.

SMITH, Joan, age 6, died 8 Dec 1941, daughter of Sto. James Smith, R.N., and of Henrietta Smith. Died at 57 Tarset Street.

SMITH, Robert, age 27, died 25 Apr 1941, 12 Guildford Place, Heaton. Died at 12 Guildford Place.

SNELL, John Henry, age 76, died 21 May 1941, Injured 25 April 1941, at Headlam Street, Willington Quay-on-Tyne; died at Royal Victoria Infirmary.

SNOWDON, Edwin, age 17, died 25 Apr 1941, 15 Guildford Place, Heaton. Son of Victor and Nora Snowdon. Died at 15 Guildford Place.

SNOWDON, Henry, age 12, died 25 April 1941, 15 Guildford Place, Heaton. Son of Victor and Nora Snowdon. Died at 15 Guildford Place.

SNOWDON, Nora, age 46, died 25 Apr 1941, 15 Guildford Place, Heaton. Daughter of the late Alexander Henry and Jessie Rita White; wife of Victor Snowdon. Died at 15 Guildford Place.

SNOWDON, Victor, age 48, died 25 Apr 1941, 15 Guildford Place, Heaton. Son of Luke William and Isabella Snowdon, of Bayswater Road, Jesmond; husband of Nora Snowdon. Died at 15 Guildford Place.

SPENCE, Sylvia, age 10, died 4 May 1942, daughter of Herbert Spence, of 40 South View, Craghead, Co. Durham. Injured 1 May 1942, at Beamish, Co. Durham; died at General Hospital.

STEPHENSON, Mary, age 31, died 2 Sept 1941, 6 Argyle Place. Wife of Pte. James Stephenson, Royal Army Ordnance Corps. Injured at 6 Argyle Place; died same day at Royal Victoria Infirmary.

STUART, Katharine Winifred, age 25, died 29 Dec 1941, M.B., B.S. Daughter of Dr. and Mrs. Frederick Joshua Stuart, of Kenros, Wellingborough Road, Weston Favell, Northampton. Died at rear of Keyes Gardens.

THOMPSON, Charles Thomas, age 62, died 25 Apr 1941, Home Guard; of 86A Heaton Road. Husband of Margaret Isabella Thompson. Died at 86A Heaton Road.

TULIP, John Scott, age 32, died 31 May 1941, Fireman, A.F.S. Son of Mr. and Mrs. Tulip, of 30 Priory Street, Byker; husband of Mary Davison Tulip, of 2 St. Ann's Row, City Road. Injured at Tarset Street, Battlefield, died same day at Royal Victoria Infirmary.

TURNER, James, age 37, died 29 Dec 1941, son of the late James Turner, of 103 Sandringham Road, South Gosforth; husband of Agnes Turner. Died at 41 Matthew Bank, Jesmond.

VASHKEVICH, Anthony, age 62, died 21 Oct 1941, 1014 Shields Road. Husband of Isabella Vashkevich. Died at 1014 Shields Road.

VENUS, David Harkus, age 27, died 25 Apr 1941, of 12 Guildford Place, Heaton. Died at 12 Guildford Place.

WALKER, Gertrude, age 34, died 1 May 1942, W.V.S.; of Morningside, Benton Park Road. Daughter of Alfred Ernest Barker, of Alba House, Woodlands, Gosforth, and of the late Gertrude Alice Barker; wife of John Walton Walker. Died at Benton Park Road.

WALLACE, Joseph, age 74, died 2 Sept 1941, husband of Mary Elizabeth Wallace, of 45 Clarence Street. Died at Robson's Woodyard, St. Peter's.

WALTON, Jane Whitworth, age 15, died 2 Sept 1941, 17 Turner Street, Shieldfield. Daughter of Andrew Walton. Injured 1 September 1941, at 17 Turner Street; died at Royal Victoria Infirmary.

WANDLESS, John, age 27, died 2 Sept 1941, Fireman, N.F.S. Son of Mr. and Mrs. M. Y. Wandless, of 43 Devonshire Place, Jesmond; husband of Muriel Louise Wandless, of the same address. Died at General Hospital.

WANLESS, George, age 30, died 31 May 1941, Fireman, N.F.S. Husband of Mary Jane Wanless, of 96 Evistones Gardens, St. Anthony's, Walker. Died at Red Barnes, Crawhall Road.

WARDLE, Laurence, age 53, died 9 Jan 1943, A.R.P. Rescue Service, Fire Guard. Son of Thomas and Mary Wardle, of Whitehaven; husband of Grace Wardle, of 49 Newbold Street. Injured at Walker Road; died same day at Royal Victoria Infirmary.

WEALLANS, Mary, age 23, died 1 Sept 1941, 17 Turner Street, Shieldfield. Wife of Alfred Weallans. Died at 17 Turner Street.

WEALLANS, Maureen, age 2, died 2 Sept 1941, 17 Turner Street, Shieldfield. Daughter of Alfred Weallans, and of Mary Weallans. Injured 1 September 1941 at 17 Turner Street; died at Royal Victoria Infirmary.

WHITBY, Bertram James, age 45, died 3 Sept 1941, 4 Ventnor Avenue. Son of Elizabeth and George Whitby, of 6 Lower Pyke Street, Barry, South Wales; husband of Maud E. Whitby. Injured 1 September 1941, at 4 Ventnor Avenue; died at General Hospital.

WHITE, Alexander Henry, age 54, died 25 Apr 1941, 15 Guildford Place, Heaton. Son of the late Alexander Henry and Jessie Rita White, husband of the late Isabella White. Died at 15 Guildford Place.

WHITE, Blanche, age 43, died 25 Apr 1941, 15 Guildford Place, Heaton. Daughter of the late Alexander Henry and Jessie Rita White. Died at 15 Guildford Place.

WIDDRINGTON, John William Grey, age 49, died 2 Sept 1941, husband of Eva Widdrington, of 6 Argyle Place. Died at Royal Victoria Infirmary.

WILLIAMS, George Robert, age 34, died 1 Sept 1941, husband of Dorothy E. Williams, of 4 Flint Mill, Jesmond Vale. Died at Sandyford Road.

WOOD, Joseph Ross, age 11, died 1 Sept 1941, son of Sjt. Joseph R. Wood, The Gordon Highlanders, and J. Wood, of 22 Togston Crescent, North Broomhill. Died at 44 Athol Street.

WRIGHT, Elizabeth, age 53, died 1 Sept 1941, 125 Union Road, Byker. Daughter of the late William and Janet Wright, of 7 Ford Street, Byker. Died at Union Road.

WRIGHT, Mary, age 31, died 1 Sept 1941, 125 Union Road, Byker. Daughter of Elizabeth Wright. Died at Union Road.

WRIGHT, William Francis, age 41, died 3 Jan 1942, son of William R. and Sarah A. Wright, of 205 Kendal Street, Byker; husband of Catherine Wright, of 8 Gladstone Street, Beeston, Nottingham. Injured 29 December 1941, at Newcastle; died at Royal Victoria Infirmary.

YOUNG, David, age 3, died 1 Sept 1941, 22 Togston Crescent, North Broomhill. Son of Pte. Alexander Young, Pioneer Corps. Died at 44 Athol Street.

Select Bibliography and Further Reading

Anon, *Meet the Members: A Record of the Timber Corps* (Bristol 1945)

Armstrong, Craig *Newcastle at War 1939-1945* (Barnsley 2019)

Armstrong, Craig *Tyneside in the Second World War* (Stroud 2007)

Barclay, C. N. *History of the Royal Northumberland Fusiliers in the Second World War* (London 1952)

Berriman, Geoffrey *County Durham and Northumberland During the Second World War* (Seaham 2005)

Clay, Ewart Waide *The Path of the 50th (Northumbrian) Division in the Second World War* (London 1950)

Collier, Basil *The Defence of the United Kingdom* (HMSO London 1957)

Delaforce, Patrick *The Polar Bears, Monty's Left Flank: From Normandy to the Relief of Holland with the 49th Division* (Stroud 1995)

Fleming, Peter *Invasion 1940* (London 1959)

Hardy, Clive and Harris, Paul *Tyneside at War* (Manchester 1988)

Hayward, James *Myths and Legends of the Second World War* (Stroud 2006)

Lampe, David *The Last Ditch: Britain's Secret Resistance and the Nazi Invasion Plan* (London 2007)

Sackville-West, Vita *The Women's Land Army* (London 1944)

Sobo, Muriel *Land Girls of Northumberland 1940-1950* (Newcastle 2003)

Storey, Neil *Northumberland's Military Heritage* (Stroud 2017)

Storey, Neil and Kay, Fiona *Women in the Second World War* (Stroud 2019)

Tegner, Henry *The Story of a Regiment: The Northumberland Hussars* (Gateshead 1969)

Todd, Nigel *In Excited Times* (Whitley Bay 1995)

Torday, Jane *Wish Me Luck As You Wave Me Goodbye: A Selection of Northumbrian Memories of World War II* (Newcastle 1989)

Whitehead, Capt. A. P. *Harder than Hammers* (Perth 1947)

Newspapers and Periodicals
Newcastle Chronicle
Newcastle Evening Chronicle
Newcastle Journal and North Mail
St George's Gazette
The Times

Useful websites
North-East Diary 1939-1945 by Roy Ripley and Brian Pears ne-diary.genuki.uk/index.html

North East War Memorials Project
www.newmp.org.uk/

Commonwealth War Graves Commission
www.cwgc.org

Acknowledgements

The author would also like to acknowledge the contributions made by numerous veterans of the Second World War and their families who have shared their memories, memoirs, photographs and memorabilia with the author over the years, especially the family of Heaton soldier the late WO II Billy Chape, 505 Field Regiment, Royal Engineers.

We would also like to add our personal thanks to Alan Kay, Ian Johnson, Marc Hope, Peter Hasselby David Hepworth, Derek Tree and all our pals in the Tyneside Scottish past and present

Neil R Storey is an award winning historian who has made a specialised study on the impact of war on British society in the 20th century. He has published over forty books and has produced countless articles for national magazines and journals. He has a nationally respected archive of original social and military history photographs and ephemera, he lectures for both social and academic audiences all over the UK. Neil regularly appears as guest expert on television and radio factual programmes.

Fiona Kay is a born and bred Geordie girl and proud of it. She lives in Northumberland and has known the county all her life. Fiona has had a life-long interest in social history and has amassed a remarkable collection of North East social history and fashion photographs to illustrate her books and talks. She is a researcher with both a keen eye and empathy with the past. Fiona has worked on both national and local history projects making history interactive and accessible for all ages.